A Man Escaped

A Man Escaped

André Devigny

Translated from the French
by Peter Green

Introduction by
Patrick Marnham

The Lyons Press
Guilford, Connecticut

An imprint of The Globe Pequot Press

First Lyons Press edition, 2002

The Lyons Press is an imprint of The Globe Pequot Press.

First published in the United States of America
by Random House, 1958.

Published in Great Britain under the title *Escape from Montluc.*

Translated from the French title *Un Condamné à Mort S'est Echappé*

Printed in Canada

2   4   6   8   10   9   7   5   3   1

ISBN 1-58574-572-3

The Library of Congress Cataloging-in-Publication Data
is available on file.

Introduction
by Patrick Marnham

In the epic of the French Resistance, André Devigny is remembered as a warrior, one of that small minority who lived out the popular idea of resistance as armed combat. At the out break of war in 1939, this former athlete and schoolteacher became an officer in an elite regiment, the Chasseurs Alpins. After France's defeat in 1940, he taught himself to become a saboteur and an assassin.

Devigny was the head of the "Gilbert" resistance network. He was arrested in April 1943, three days after killing Mussolini's police chief in the occupied city of Nice. His network had earlier been responsible for attacking a munitions factory in Toulouse. But one of its members, Robert Moog, an Alsatian French citizen who had been recruited by German military intelligence, the Abwehr, infiltrated this group—and it was he who ultimately betrayed Devigny.

After his arrest, Devigny was interrogated and tortured by his German and French captors. One of his fellow prisoners said, "they half-killed him." Instead of breaking his spirit, this treatment had the opposite effect and made Devigny more determined to continue the fight. André Devigny was a member of a right-wing resistance movement, and he makes it clear that his Catholic faith was part of the reason why he was able to continue his resistance work. Throughout his ordeal he never became brutalized; he even confessed to being troubled by the killing of the Nice police chief, and recalls that while he lay on Death Row his dreams were haunted by his victim's face.

About six weeks after entering Montluc, Devigny glimpsed a horrifying sight, a face with "hollow eyes . . . a thick, black, blood-stained beard and long tangled hair," and then realized that he was looking at his own reflection in a mirror. He had to all appearances become just another lost soul, waiting to hear his name on the morning roll call, "with" or "without" baggage. "With baggage" meant "Night and Fog," deportation to a concentration camp and oblivion somewhere within the Reich. "Without" meant immediate death, a firing squad in front of a prison wall or in a ditch outside. But Devigny was not prepared to join the ranks of the Gestapo's living dead. He wanted to die "facing the enemy, so that his children would know that their father had never lost heart or surrendered." Among his fellow prisoners there was de Pury, a Protestant minister who helped him to live with his uneasy conscience, Jeantet, a suicidal loner who was contemptuously uninterested in Resistance, and Nathan, who was in fact Roger Nathan, a swimming international and a Jewish freemason who was eventually deported to Buchenwald. The fact that this ill-assorted group should have become the close friends of the right-wing Catholic army officer shows us how, on the front line of Resistance, among those the French called "les petits soldats," the bitter ideological and political arguments of the leadership were irrelevant.

When Devigny escaped from death row in Fort Montluc, three days before the date set for his execution, it caused a sensation. Escapes from German custody in France during the Occupation were rare, and particularly so from Montluc, which was reputed to be escape-proof. Despite attempts to conceal the news, rumors quickly spread around Lyons, a city in which the name of Montluc inspired dread, the fear of torture, and the death of hope. The prison was used to hold not only resisters but also Jews awaiting deportation, as well as petty criminals and men suspected of black market activities. Built as a military prison for 130 men, it had been closed for sanitary reasons before the outbreak of war. The Gestapo re-opened it; Montluc could have been designed for their purposes. Devigny makes little of the conditions inside the prison; he mentions the absence of silence, the lack of food, the smell, and the lice. Other prisoners remembered that Montluc was literally crawling with vermin, the bedbugs dropped from cracks in the ceilings onto the inmates at night. During the Occupation, its prisoner population rose as high as 1,500.

In A MAN ESCAPED, Devigny's account of prison life is the more convincing for being so unexpected. He eventually broke-out with his cell companion who was in the LVF, the body of French volunteers raised to fight with the German army, and who was still wearing the rags of his uniform. And the German military commandant of Montluc, Franzel, a brutally violent man who had been a circus ringmaster in civilian life, was also an anti-Nazi who allowed favored prisoners to have regular family contacts within the prison walls, and who lived in dread of the Gestapo's visits. The Gestapo remains a shadowy presence in the book just as they did in fact. Writing in 1956, Devigny was still uncertain of the identity of his chief adversary, the head of the Gestapo in Lyons. So SS Lieut. Klaus Barbie, who was eventually tried and convicted of crimes against humanity in 1987, appears in the book as "Colonel Barbier."

Reflecting on the ruthless energy he had dedicated to his escape, Devigny later compared himself to "a hunted animal." His readers may look on him as a little higher than that, though. He always knew that even if he escaped he would pay a high price, and in due course when the Gestapo failed to recapture him, they deported members of his family instead. When A MAN ESCAPED was first published, it was immediately recognized as a classic of war literature. The film of the book won a prize at the Cannes Film Festival in 1957, by which time Devigny had been named a Compagnon de la Libération, France's top wartime decoration. But perhaps his real achievement was to have given so many of his fellow countrymen the strength to fight on.

A Man Escaped

1

We were waiting for Angrisani near the garden of his villa, a few feet away from the front gate.

Muller whispered: "He's not coming. Let's get back to Nice."

"There's a light in the hall. He wouldn't be late if he could help it."

It was a beautiful night in mid-April. The moon was shining in a clear sky, and countless stars glittered above us. The only cover was the slight shadow cast by some high bushes near the garden gate; hardly enough to conceal both of us. From some way off, the far side of the road, came the measured roar of waves breaking on the beach. At least it drowned the quick beating of our hearts. The lights in the house next door went out one after the other. We became more and more conscious of our loneliness, more nervous as the fatal moment approached. Occasionally a car sped by; each time I listened as it approached, and shook my head.

I said: "Don't worry. He'll come."

I hated this job. It gave me sleepless nights and nagged at me all day. I had killed men before, but openly, as a soldier. On December 16, 1939, for instance, I killed the German captain who was leading the attack on my position; but then I was myself in command of an infantry company. We fought according to the rules. I was wearing uniform; I was not alone. Instead of this oppressive silence we had a battlefield, with all its noisy confusion: exploding shells, whining bullets, smoke, shouting. I was keyed up by the responsibility of command, the need to set an example, the atmosphere natural to armed combat. We had to destroy the enemy; not only our position, but our lives and freedom depended on doing so.

But here we had to face our duty alone. Roland Netter had had a brilliant record during the first two years of the war, and had been decorated three times; yet a week before, at the exact moment when I had given the order to attack, he had failed me. After I had jumped out of our hiding-place to go in behind the car, I looked back—luckily—to see if he was following me. He had not moved; I was alone. I scarcely had time to hide behind the pillared portico while Angrisani shut the gates. A few moments later I went back to Netter. I found him trembling and drenched in sweat. He whispered: "It's too much for me; I can't do it."

But it had to be done, whatever the cost it had to be done; those were our orders. If only we had been able to argue the pros and cons, slip stealthily away, put the operation off till later! But no; now more than ever our standing orders were stamped in my mind. *On these operations there can be no turning back: success or death.*

Muller, on the other hand, doubted neither me nor himself. His trust in my leadership was so implicit that my presence alone was sufficient guarantee for him: any mission, however hazardous, was bound to succeed. We had first met in Morocco, and later shared a room at the military training college in Aix-en-Provence.

I know nothing so productive of close and abiding friendship as a soldier's life; and Muller, with his powerful physique, eager expression and pleasant, even nature, inspired immediate sympathy. He was naturally drawn to the active rather than the contemplative life, and felt more at home on a field exercise than in the lecture-room. These tastes I also shared; and this drew us still closer together. He was delighted to join our organisation: it gave him the chance to "do something" at last.

Colonel Groussard, who commanded the group, gave him the

job of watching the ports of Marseilles and Toulon. The confidence which such an appointment implied was fully justified. He very quickly succeeded in establishing agents throughout his area. Every week his reports arrived in Lyons, at Dr. Bacharach's house, which was used as an accommodation address. He accepted this Nice mission without any hesitation, and at once made meticulous preparations for it. He personally constructed a bludgeon from a lump of lead which he sewed into a leather sheath and fixed on the end of a stout stick. He had also managed to obtain a small nickel-plated revolver, which reminded me of a child's toy.

Meanwhile I had contacted Eugene Laidevant, a police inspector who was a member of our organisation. He lent me a revolver and a rubber blackjack. I also possessed a dagger; but Pierre Ponchardier, the naval commander with whom I was staying in Nice, pointed out that its blade was too large for this kind of job. He gave me instead a Chinese stiletto, which he had picked up during a cruise in the Far East.

On the day of the operation we met to discuss final details in the Café Masséna, about the middle of the afternoon. Then we settled down at a convenient observation-point near the Boulevard Carnot. There was a splendid view of the mountains behind the city, and the sea that day was wonderfully blue and calm.

But we could not take our eyes off the luxurious house which lay below us. For more than an hour we waited, leaning on the railings beside the road.

A maid hung up washing to dry in the garden. A car arrived, and left again: Angrisani, no doubt. He was constantly in my thoughts. Angrisani: commandant of the Italian police in this area. Now this cruel and legendary figure would have to pay for his countless crimes; and it was I who had to destroy him, in a fashion for which I felt considerable distaste. It was unpleasant; but I had no choice. Colonel Groussard had ordered me to direct the operation without taking an active part in it; but, for various reasons, all those I had approached had failed me. I would have to do it myself, whatever the cost.

We finally walked down into Nice at nightfall, and arranged a rendezvous outside the villa shortly before midnight.

And here we still were, waiting.

Suddenly a car slowed down and turned off the main highway on to the gravelled lane. Its headlights slashed the darkness above our heads. It pulled up opposite the entrance to the house, engine idling. Muller moved towards it. I heard his laboured breathing. We were flat on our bellies, only our heads raised.

Angrisani got out, took a bunch of keys from his pocket, opened the gates, walked into the courtyard and opened the garage. Then he turned the garage light on and came back to his car. I gave Muller the signal at the precise moment the big Lancia began to move again. We sprang up and ran for the gateway. Bent double, we followed the car in, Muller on the left, myself on the right. Through the rear window I could observe every least move our man made.

The car stopped. The Italian switched off engine and headlights. He half-opened the door and eased himself slowly out of his seat, on my side. He stretched himself, a big, heavy, powerful figure, and whistled a little tune as he walked. I saw his back clearly, closer to me now; then his head. I took one step forward and gave him a smashing blow with my blackjack, full on the skull. My weapon jumped out of my hand with the shock of the blow, and Angrisani's spectacles flew into the air.

He roared with pain, turned, flung up his arms and came for me, howling like a beast. I jumped back to hit him the easier. He tried to get a grip on my shoulders; as I stepped aside Muller fired from the cover of the car. The bullet caught Angrisani beside the ear just as I drove my stiletto into his breast. He fell on his face, gasping faintly still. I pressed the muzzle of my revolver down on the top of his head, and pulled the trigger. The whole business only took a few seconds.

But Angrisani's cries, and the two shots, had made a good deal of noise. On such a still night they could hardly fail to be heard. We could not count on escaping in the car; and anyway, it would have taken far too long to go through Angrisani's pockets for the ignition key, shift his huge hulking corpse out of our way, start the engine, and find out how the gears worked. The odds on our getting away in so well-known a car were also somewhat doubtful.

So we made off for Nice on foot as fast as we could. Some woman shouted "Help, murder!" out of a window. About fifty yards from the villa we passed a Revenue post, and the officer on duty came out.

"What's going on?"

"I don't know," I said. We quickened our pace and went on down the road.

As we ran we agreed to fight it out if they tried to arrest us, however many there were of them.

Down at the port an Italian sentry was on guard. As we passed by I called out good night to him in his own language, and he replied cheerfully.

I told Muller it would be wiser for us to separate. We shook hands and went our own ways.

Three days later, April 17, 1943, as I was walking out of An-nemasse station, strong hands gripped me and hustled me into a waiting car.

I was in the hands of the German secret police.

Slowly, carefully, I moved my arm, put my hand on the door handle and pushed it a little. It made no noise, but I felt it give. I knew it would be easy enough to open when the right moment came. For the moment I sank back in the apathetic attitude of my two fellow-prisoners.

Newton caught my eye; he had guessed what I meant to do. On the front seats the driver and S.S. sergeant were chatting away, paying no attention to us. How had I been lucky enough not to be handcuffed? I did not waste time on surprise; I only knew that I had to use my luck. Today, April 23, was to mark my first attempt at escape.

Nearly a week earlier, on the day after my arrest, I had arrived in Lyons. I was weak from the interrogations I had undergone, from lack of food, from sheer physical exhaustion. I only had a glimpse of a huge bare wall that exuded hostility. Ellers, Timann, and Moog, my interrogators, had woken me up and quickly dragged me out of the car. I had managed to sleep during the journey, even though my wrists were handcuffed together behind my back.

I had been hustled down corridors and through doors till we came to a soldier who took the laces out of my shoes, removed my tie and belt, and made an inventory of what I had in my pockets. Then, at last, I reached my cell. Number 13. Good or bad luck? I fell on the skimpy straw mattress and lay there, face downwards, because of the handcuffs, trying in vain to sleep.

I spent some hours trying to work out a system of defence against interrogation. Then they sent for me again. It looked like an unpleasant day.

Now the car had just passed Perrache station. We were following the river towards Montluc, and going too fast for me to jump out. Muscles tensed, ready for action, I tried to distract myself by studying my companions. I had met many new faces during the last few days, but in a sense they were all the same face: profoundly sad, with lined cheeks, unkempt hair and half-grown beard.

In prison we assembled silently, down a long corridor; we were forbidden to exchange a single word while we were being chained together.

This scene, simple though it was, and of daily occurrence, took on a solemn, almost ritual character. Over everyone hung the uncertainty of what tomorrow might bring; we all suffered from uneasy fear and the effects of our solitary confinement. Alone, we chewed over our thoughts again and again: the cud of past and future alike. When our wretched column moved off, it was to the headquarters of the Gestapo at the Station Hotel. There was always an S.S. sergeant shouting *kommen!* or *los!* at us, bullying, never leaving us in peace for a single moment.

On this particular morning the truck had come to the prison for us very early. Haggard, exhausted (often we lay awake nearly till dawn) we formed up as usual. In the Station Hotel they left us in a room which was completely bare except for a few chairs along the walls. I remained there the whole morning without being interrogated. Perhaps this was one way of trying to undermine our morale.

These hours of waiting were, I must admit, nerve-racking. Despite myself, I listened for the noise of footsteps in the corridor outside, wondering again and again if the moment had come. The moment when I should have to face Moog, the German agent who had penetrated our organisation and found out everything I was doing. The moment when I should once more have to fight against the effects of beatings and torture. The moment when I must deny, deny everything—my journeys across the frontier, the sabotaging of the explosives factory in Toulouse, the Nice business, everything.

It must have been one o'clock before the sergeant who had escorted me took me downstairs again. Walking in front of him, I went through the hotel vestibule and out into a black Citroën. Two prisoners were already in the back: Pierre Perrin and Alfred Newton. Newton was an English captain who had tried to escape a day or two before. He had jumped, wearing handcuffs, from the third floor of the Station Hotel. The glass roof above the veranda had broken his fall. The Germans recaptured him immediately; he had broken one arm and dislocated his collar-bone. Now he was in plaster of Paris and wore a sling.

I was quite sure he knew what I intended to do, and approved of it. But all the way along the road by the river we never slowed down. I sat hunched up, ready to jump, anxiously watching the familiar route. We were nearly back at the prison now, and the car was still going at full speed. Was I going to miss this unique opportunity?

The two Germans still chatted cheerfully; the road remained depressingly clear. There was nothing to pull them up. My hopes faded as the riverside wharfs flashed past.

It was quite near the prison, just before we reached the railway bridge, that I took my chance. I acted by pure instinct, almost involuntarily. A tram was crossing the bridge, and our driver braked. Quickly and neatly I twisted the handle, threw the door open, and jumped. I had rehearsed this act a dozen times. I went rolling over in the road, thrown off balance. In a flash I scrambled to my feet and crossed to the other side of the road.

I began to run as fast as I could, hugging the wall, drawing on an unsuspected reserve of energy. On I went, dodging from side to side. They were bound to try and shoot me down.

I was gaining on them—at least I guessed as much, because I dared not look round. Frantically I ran on; the wall looked as though it would go on for ever. Then several shots rang out; a bullet went through the sleeve of my coat and grazed my arm.

Where was this attack coming from? Not from my guards, clearly; they could not have got so close. Without stopping, I glanced over my shoulder. A car was following me, cruising slowly. Several German officers were leaning out of the windows and firing at me. They were only a dozen yards away.

Trapped between the car and this blind wall, I knew my attempt had failed. I raised my arms above my head and stood quite still. The officers had already got hold of me when the S.S. guards ran up shouting, enormously relieved at my recapture. They half-dragged, half-carried me back to the truck, cuffing and shoving me as they went. A large crowd of civilians, attracted by the shooting and yelling, watched me pass. What they felt I can only guess; but there was nothing they could do. I had had my chance, and now Fate was turning against me. The officers who had intercepted me were air force pilots coming into Lyons from their station; it was pure bad luck that they had appeared where and when they did.

I got into the seat next to Newton that I had left so abruptly a few minutes before. My escort thanked the air force officers effusively for their help, and then turned furiously on me. He leant his weight on my knees and handcuffed me, wrenching my wrists brutally.

Then he took his pistol by the barrel and began to batter me round the head with it, cursing me as he did so. The butt made deep wounds in my scalp; I felt warm blood stream down my forehead and cheeks. I bore his attack in silence, waiting till his anger died down. Newton was watching me in agonised sympathy; I thought I saw the word *courage!* shape itself on his lips.

When it was over, I passed my manacled hands over my face; they came away all bloody. This time I was sure I should be shot as soon as we got back to Montluc. In the courtyard, near the kitchens, the sergeant left me for a few moments. The news of my attempted escape spread rapidly. Soldiers gathered round me in a hostile circle, and began to kick me about. Resigned to the worst, I retreated till I had my back to the wall, waiting to be led before the firing squad.

Anyone who has been in Montluc Prison must remember Fränzel, the Head Warder. No one could forget that squat, corpulent figure, that square head, those steel-rimmed glasses; much less his angry voice and continual oaths. I doubted if he had ever learnt to talk; his only language consisted of curses and blows.

He appeared now, accompanied by two of his men. They seized me by the shoulders and dragged me off to the blacksmith's shop, a small building in the corner of the court behind the kitchens. They tore off first the handcuffs, then my coat and shoes, threw me over the anvil, and beat me in turn with pick-handles. I knew I should get no mercy from them; when Fränzel drew his revolver and pushed it in my face I thought my last moment had come. His finger whitened on the trigger, and I shut my eyes. Why he did not fire I shall never know. Instead he spat in my face; an act which defiled me more than a bullet could ever have done.

I began to scream, conscious now of my bruised and aching body. I knew that I could in fact stand up under such treatment for a long time; so I pretended to faint, letting myself slide down to the ground and lie completely motionless.

2

The Head Warder had me taken to one of the condemned cells. I was thrown down on the straw mattress, and my bleeding wrists were once more handcuffed. The door clanged to behind me.

I half-opened one bleary eye and saw that the light which usually shone through the spy-hole in the door was now blocked. Fränzel was still watching me.

At length his heavy footsteps echoed away down the corridor, accompanied by the unpleasant sound of clinking keys. There was absolute silence; something extremely rare in Montluc.

The reason was plain enough. My screams and Fränzel's curses must have been audible from the courtyard. I realised that the other prisoners understood what I had just gone through: sensed their unspoken compassion. In this silence each one of them, shut up alone, felt his own misery reflected in mine.

With Fränzel gone, an enormous sense of relief spread through me. At last I was alone. I was free to think, to rally my mental resources. I could let my mind dwell at leisure on my home and family. I had not been shot out of hand; clearly Fränzel had to report the incident to the Gestapo and await their orders. But there was no doubt I would die the following morning. It would have been better to have got it over at once, in the car or down in the courtyard. I had been ready to die then; summary execution was something I understood.

Suddenly the silence was broken by several quiet taps, a dozen or more, against the wall of my cell. They were muffled by the thickness of the wall itself, but clearly audible. I had, it seemed, a neighbour; a fellow-sufferer in the adjoining cell. I knocked with my handcuffs against the concrete; my unseen friend replied. Then I lay back on my mattress, and withdrew to the solitude of my thoughts. I had had such abominable luck today, and my nerves were worn so raw with physical and emotional suffering that I had no capacity to respond. At such a moment the knowledge that a friend was near gave me no relief. I was not worried by the situation I found myself in; my courage had never failed me yet, and I was convinced it would last me to the end. What I could not bear was the agony which my wife would suffer if I died, the lonely task she would have of bringing up our three children without help. Tenderness welled up in me: I lay for a long time in silent torment. I got no evening meal, and never noticed its absence.

My shirt was glued to my lacerated skin, and clotted blood thickened in my hair and eight-day beard. I could still move my legs and arms; clearly the punishment I had undergone had not damaged me too badly. All the same, I was in a nasty state.

I fell into a deep and exhausted sleep.

The heavy tramp of feet woke me. It was early morning.

This is it, I thought. You are going to be shot, and you wasted your last night on earth asleep.

"God," I whispered, "give me courage."

The door opened. Timann and Moog came in, in civilian clothes. Behind them were Fränzel and the sergeant we called *Komm-Komm*, from whom I had escaped the day before. These two were in uniform. Timann came over to my mattress and looked at me. I stared back, not lowering my eyes.

"Get up," he said.

I pretended to have great difficulty in moving, and whimpered with pain at each step I took. Fränzel stood over the bedstead and kicked me. I fell to my knees and dragged myself across to the opposite wall. Here I tottered to my feet, dragging one leg as if it hurt me to move it at all, and keeping my manacled hands pressed against the wall. He thrust me back into the middle of the cell with brutal violence.

The key turned in the lock, footsteps moved away down the corridor. The heavy steel door which cut off the condemned block from the rest of the prison slammed shut. I was alone once more. For a moment I stood there, trembling, unable to credit this second reprieve. Slowly, as my terror ebbed away, life flowed back into my veins. My neighbour rapped on his cell-wall to make sure I was still there. I replied at once, and felt myself grow calmer.

The beating I had taken the previous evening had left me stiff and weak. The wounds in my scalp were still hurting badly, and the blood which had clotted inside my nose had made it swell up in a disgusting fashion. All the same, no serious damage had been done. I prodded myself all over, flexed my legs and arms, and even managed to get a handkerchief out of my pocket to mop up the open cuts which marked my body. I lay down on the mattress, and began to think of my family and the valley in Savoy where we had lived. My eyes remained wide open.

Several shrill blasts on a whistle and the shouting of many voices woke me from this reverie. The prison was coming to life: morning was here. I heard sounds of life coming from every floor of the building: the clang of slop-pails on stone flags, clattering mess-tins. These familiar noises did me good; I felt less cut off in an atmosphere which had some association with life as I knew it.

The steel door creaked open again. Each cell was opened in turn; through my spy-hole I saw a soldier put a mess-tin in the one opposite mine, and an N.C.O. lock the door again. As on the previous evening, I got nothing.

Later that morning a warder came into my cell alone. He pushed me out into the corridor, took off my handcuffs, and made me walk towards the ablutions, a machine-pistol pressed in the small of my back. The ablutions were down the corridor, just this side of the iron door. With the help of my one handkerchief I washed my face and dabbed some water on my wounds. I stayed there a little while longer to take a good drink of water and shake my shirt out. The German stood in the doorway; he made no attempt to hinder me, but watched every move I made. I limped back to my cell. It was the end one on the left. The warder carefully manacled me again and locked the door on me. Then I heard him open the next one, and my invisible neighbour took my place in the ablutions.

Those few moments spent outside, and the cold water, had done me a great deal of good. I put my handkerchief to dry on a little concrete ledge that was fixed to the wall in one corner of my cell, below the fanlight. Then I neatly re-made my bed, laid out my clothes and shoes, and once more relaxed in a kind of day-dream. My eyes were fixed on the tiny patch of blue sky which showed through the thick bars fixed in my window.

Towards the end of the morning I got up, driven by a tremendous urge to move my limbs, to exercise myself. Two paces; a half-turn. Two paces; a half-turn. I went on like this for about five minutes. Then I tried to reach the edge of the fanlight by scrambling up on the cement ledge. It wasn't easy. My manacles were a handicap, and at first I failed altogether. In the end I had to stand my wooden bedstead up against the wall. It was a delicate operation.

I looked cautiously through the fanlight. At the same time I was listening for approaching footsteps in the corridor, ready to jump down at the least hint of danger.

Three men in plain clothes, washed and shaved, were walking up and down a large square cobbled courtyard. At one end I could see a wash-house and latrines. They walked as far as the wash-house and then turned back, passing close under my fanlight.

On the left was a row of large barred windows. On the right a wall about ten feet high divided this first courtyard from a smaller one. At the far end of the second courtyard I could see the tiled roof of a covered gallery. I memorised all this quickly, and then drew in my head and listened. I heard nothing unusual. I stayed where I was for a little longer, breathing in the warm sunny air. It was a beautiful day.

One of the men below seemed considerably older than the others.

What little hair he had left was completely white; he must have been at least fifty-five, I thought. Were they prisoners? If so, why were they on their own? Should I draw their attention to me? If they looked up and examined the angle of the wall carefully they ought to be able to see me.

I decided to risk it. What had I got to lose now?

As they passed beneath me I whistled softly, twice. They heard the noise, looked up, and saw me.

"Who are you?" asked one of them in a low voice.

"A French officer."

"What is your name?"

"Devigny. I escaped yesterday."

"How?"

"Jumped out of a moving car. But they caught me again immediately."

"So it *is* you! You screamed so much when you were beaten we thought you were dead. Wait a minute. We'd better walk round the courtyard again."

While they were doing this I listened for movements in the corridor. But everything was quiet.

"Where are you from?" he asked.

"Haute-Savoie."

"Do your family know you're here?"

"No."

"Have you anything to write on?"

"No. Only a handkerchief."

"I'll get you a pencil and some paper tomorrow."

"You mean you can get letters out?"

"Yes. See you tomorrow."

I remained motionless, amazed, unable to believe in such a miracle. I could not take my eyes off this man. With one word he had brought me hope and dissolved my despair. Then I heard a sound inside. I jumped down quickly and replaced my bedstead in its corner. The warders were handing out soup to my neighbours. Yet again I was left without food; it was now over forty-eight hours since I had eaten. But, much more important, I was in a state bordering on happiness.

I had been in this hellish place for a week now. I had become a puppet in the hands of men who lacked the least grain of humanity in their make-up. I had been racked with pain, terror, and the fear of the unknown; I had reached the last depths of despair. Now this apparently friendly figure had uttered a few magic words; and as a result my elation was such that I forgot both my bruised body and starved, growling stomach.

You mean you can get letters out?

Yes.

I repeated the words over and over again. I needed to convince myself that I hadn't been the victim of some hallucination. He had been so surprised to see me and hear my voice, there had been such sympathy on his face, that I could not bring myself to disbelieve him. The chance he had offered me to get a message through to the outside world—only a few hours after my terrible experience that morning—seemed a real miracle. I lay down on my bed, happy now.

Several quick taps on the wall. My neighbour was there. It was the middle of the afternoon. I replied at once. Then came three measured knocks, a pause, and one single knock afterwards. It was obviously a code, and I guessed the way it worked very quickly: one tap for each letter, a short pause to divide them, a longer pause to break up words. Three taps meant C; one stood for A.

"*Ça va?*" he asked.

"*Ça va.*"

"Name?"

"Devigny. And yours?"

"Ruffet. Home?"

"Savoy. Yours?"

"Lyons."

I asked him what his job was.

"Sheet-metal worker," he replied.

"Age?"

"Nineteen. And you?"

"Twenty-six."

"Condemned?"

"No. Are you?"

"Yes. To death. French tribunal."

"How long here?"

"Three weeks."

"Any other prison?"

"Yes. Saint-Paul."

"Where?"

"Lyo—"

There was a sound in the corridor, and the conversation abruptly broke off. I used the break to pull out a twig from the broom I had in my cell. With this I could count out each letter on the white-washed wall and remember everything he told me. When all was quiet again we recommenced our dialogue. I learnt that the poor fellow had been arrested by the French police for the murder of a German soldier. They had condemned him to death, but he had been taken over by the Gestapo.

"Do your family know?"

"I have no relatives."

"Hungry?"

"Yes."

"Parcels?"

"No."

It took an age to tap these words out, but what did time matter to us? Besides, we had no means of measuring it. We were in a segregated world where life outside meant nothing.

"Good night," my neighbour tapped out when the evening meal was due to be served.

"Good night." So we ended our conversation for the day: a day which had begun under the shadow of death and ended in a faint ray of hope.

That night I dreamt of a magnificent dinner. Course after course appeared, piled high with delicacies; but I remained insatiable.

I had eaten nothing for over two days now; all I had had was a

drink of tap water. Hunger was beginning to undermine my
strength; it attacked me during the night so as to sap my physical
and moral strength more subtly during the day.

April 25. Easter.
This Sunday had begun with the usual shrilling whistles; as on
the day before, there was the confused, vague babel of activity
which meant that the prison was coming to life. I got up and
folded my blankets carefully, as I always did. There were footsteps in the corridor, the clink of keys in locks, the clatter of mess-
tins. An eye peered through my spy-hole. But nothing more happened that morning. As on the previous day, I spent some time in
the wash-house after performing my ablutions. On the way back I
saw some words chalked on my door.
Kein essen 28.
Nothing to eat till the twenty-eighth, that is, till Tuesday! That
meant two more days of starvation. But this news did not disturb
me as much as it might have done; the one thing I was looking forward to was climbing up to my fanlight and talking to the friend I
had made the previous day. The minutes dragged past. I had to
wait till I heard the heavy iron door shut. It took a long time;
obviously my neighbours, too, were taking some time over their
ablutions.
I whistled softly.
"Hullo, there!"
"All right?" he asked.
"Better—thanks to you."
"Watch carefully. I'm going to throw something up to you. Try
and catch it."
Awkwardly, I thrust my manacled hands through the bars, one
above the other. After two unsuccessful attempts I managed to
catch the small packet he threw up, and at once hid it in my shirt.
"Now you have paper and a pencil. Write your letter and drop
it down to me tomorrow."
"What is your name?"
"Bury."

"Where are you from?"

"Saint-Etienne."

"Thank you. Till tomorrow."

I took another long look at this man who dared to take such risks on behalf of someone he did not know—simply because he knew they were worse off than he was. His two companions had walked on without raising their heads.

Back in the cell, I took out the little packet and examined it. There were several sheets of yellowish paper, a pencil, a pebble to act as a weight. They were all wrapped up in a piece of newspaper, a precious possession which I carefully hid.

I had the whole day in which to write this vital letter. How was I to say the countless things I wanted to in one short message? Whom should I address it to? Should I, above all, first communicate with my family or the Resistance? Robert Moog had said, while interrogating me: "Your transmitting station in Toulouse is in our hands now. We have broken the code, and we are sending false messages to the English. Perkins, your radio operator, is in prison. He'll be shot any day now."

Surely the most important thing was to warn my friends of what Moog was doing? They believed that he was one of us. Surely my duty was to let them know he was a German spy, and thus save the lives of other Resistance agents? Personal considerations could not be allowed to affect my decision. Yet if the message fell into German hands, it was not only a confession of guilt, but would mean the arrest of another member of our organisation. I must take Bury into my confidence, I thought. So I wrote two letters to start with, both addressed to Jean Cambus, a schoolmaster in Lyons.

My dear Jean,

I am in the military prison of Montluc. I enclose a letter for my parents. You know the address.

I have been interrogated for six days, but have held out. There is a German spy in our organisation—No. 37, Hitter's friend. Gilbert, Françoise's father, is not well. He must take care to stay at home. Pierre P., Lucien, and Charles are also liable to illness. Please warn them. Our hide-out has been discovered—betrayed by its watchman. Captain Bulard (954) has been killed. He leaves a wife and children.

Take care of my own family. Tell Suzanne and M. Gilbert.

This is a most important task. I am relying on you. I know you will carry it out responsibly.

I tried to escape, but failed. I was shot in the arm, put in a condemned cell, and given a terrible beating-up.

You must act quickly.

On a separate sheet I wrote this to Bury:

You have given me hope and courage at the moment when I had reached my lowest ebb. I am going to trust you. If suffering is the price we must pay for our country's freedom, I accept it gladly. I shall be at the fanlight every day. Thank you.

I wrote all this in very small handwriting, propping my bolster between my knees and folding the paper till it was thick enough to stand the pressure of the pencil. I wrapped up the letters in the piece of newspaper and hid the little packet in a crack in the bedstead.

This was my third day of fasting. The mid-day meal had been served out as usual; there had been footsteps, the noise of mess-tins, an eye peering in through the spy-hole. Nothing else.

I began to think more and more of the fine dishes my mother used to make at home. Especially my mind dwelt on those delicious pastries we eat in Savoy—brown outside and dusted with sugar, but inside all golden-yellow, rich with yolk of egg, and made with special flour.

In my imagination I ate countless such delicacies; it was, in the end, to escape from this frustrating obsession that I made contact with the occupant of the next cell. The little pebble Bury had given me proved a great help in tapping clearly on the wall.

"How are you?"

"Fine."

"Easter today."
"Yes. Do you believe in God?"
"Yes. Do you?"
"No."
"Handcuffs?"
"Yes. You can get them off."
"How?"
"Wire or a pin."
"Have you done it?"
"Yes. Press down on the ratchet-spring."
"Thanks. Good night."

That was how I spent Easter Sunday, 1943. I had written two letters and learnt that it was possible to remove these irksome handcuffs. A vast lassitude crept over me; I only felt comfortable when lying down. Starvation was having its effect on my physical strength as well as my mind. Also I was horribly thirsty. My tongue was furred, and stuck to my dry palate. I fell asleep dreaming of water—the clear spring which bubbles up in our field at home, perennial water flowing away into the depths of lush pasture.

"Ready?"
"Yes. I've got the letters here. Could you get me a pin?"
"Surely. Anything else you want?"
"Quite a lot. I've got nothing here at all, and I haven't eaten anything for four days."
"Why didn't you say so yesterday? Wait a moment. I'll be back."
He went off to the window on my left. I heard him talking to some women behind the bars. He came back and threw me up a piece of bread.
"Tomorrow you'll have everything you need."
"Thank you," I said. "Till tomorrow."
I wanted to keep a fragment of this unexpected manna for the evening, but it was impossible. I struggled to control myself for a little, pacing round my cell, fingering the bread, putting

it down again. I picked it up, intending to hide it. I tried to find good excuses for eating it all at once. In the end my will-power and good intentions were defeated. Quickly I swallowed what remained in three mouthfuls. Then I carefully gathered up, one by one, the crumbs that had dropped on the floor.

That evening a woman began to sing through one of the windows that opened on the courtyard—obviously for the benefit of the prisoners in the cells:

> Vous n'aurez pas l'Alsace et la Lorraine
> Et malgré vous . . .

As if by magic, the murmur of voices inside the prison faded to silence.

The girl's voice, soaring up clear and indomitable, embodied in those familiar words the whole symbolic essence of our struggle. Even in this grim fortress it challenged and defied the enemy. A wave of inexpressible emotion swept over me as I listened, and my courage gained fresh strength from her song.

I wanted to shout out: They can kill us, break our spirit by starvation and torture, but it makes no difference. In the end we shall get them. They will be where we are now, and we shall have our revenge.

April brought fine weather, but in this stony wilderness there was not a single tree, no scrap of green. Yet in the afternoon the sun's warm rays penetrated through the fanlights and brought a breath of spring air to our stale cells.

The spring is magnificent in Savoy, especially in the Boëge Valley. Here, as if to compensate for the cruel winter months, nature buds and blossoms in rich profusion. I pictured in my mind the flower-covered hillsides; I thought of the peaceful, slow-moving peasants who get up at dawn to sow the fields and work in the orchards.

The women had opened their windows to get the benefit of this spring air; I could hear the distant murmur of their voices as they talked to each other. Occasionally one of them called out the time. As the prisoners on the first and second floors of the block were always clamouring to know what o'clock it was, she got into the habit of giving a regular time signal.

Trams clanged down the Rue Dauphiné; trains thundered by on the nearby line; there was always a good deal of noise going on in the prison itself. As a result, I could only hear the chimes of the factory clock with great difficulty during the day. At night, on the other hand, the hours rang out slow and clear, a proof that life in the outside world continued to go on its way. I marked the days on the wall with a line, making a cross for each Sunday. In this way I kept an exact record of how time was passing.

April 28 was a notable day. Bury threw up a parcel to me which was so bulky I could hardly get it through the bars. I quickly jumped down to hide it under my bedstead, and then scrambled back to the fanlight.

I said: "Thanks for everything."

"It's from me and the women. Better now?"

"Much better. Who are the men with you?"

"Two friends from Saint-Etienne."

I found out later who they were. Blanchonnet was the editor of a paper in Lyons, and Kuster a police superintendent.

"What about my letters?"

"Don't worry; they'll be sent out. You'll be able to send some more soon."

"Good. I'll have one for you tomorrow."

"See you then."

Taking careful precautions against being caught, I opened my precious parcel. Wrapped in a napkin I found a tiny piece of soap, a bar of chocolate, some sugar, a hunk of bread and a safety-pin: treasure-trove indeed. I was particularly moved by the tiny note which accompanied these gifts: *Don't despair*, it read, *things will be better soon. We won't forget you. We'll send you a share of our parcels when we can. With love.*

How can I put my feelings into words? One has to have lived through these moments to understand how wonderful this gesture seemed in a place where torture, misery, solitude and death were the penalty for the least infringement of the rules. My emotion was due not only to the joy I felt at receiving so extraordinary a gift, but also, above all, to the sympathy and unselfish friendship of which it was the symbol.

I carefully hid the soap, the napkin, the chocolate, sugar and bread in different corners of the cell. Then I sat down on my bed, in the corner which was out of reach of the spy-hole, and began to nibble at my leisure. I took my time over it. How good everything tasted! I chewed over every crumb of that hard black bread, relishing its flavour. And then the chocolate—real milk-chocolate, wrapped in beautiful silver paper! I broke it into little pieces; each piece was delicious, despite the fur that coated my swollen tongue. The sugar was saved by the sound of approaching footsteps: a soldier opened the door, put down a spoon and a mess-tin three-quarters full of soup, and went out again. He stood watching through the spy-hole, eager to observe the spectacle of a famished man devouring his meagre rations.

I held myself back till at last I heard him move away down the corridor. Then I set about the soup.

It was wonderful soup, I thought, the work of a master chef. I ate it slowly, occasionally dipping the handle of my spoon into the mess-tin to gauge how much was left. At last I deposited the tin in the corner, licked clean, its metal interior shining impeccably. I had, I felt, swallowed ten bowls of soup, five bars of chocolate, and a whole loaf. Probably more. Certainly my first meal in five days had removed the obsessive state of mind which an empty stomach produces; I felt both physically and morally restored.

This pleasant state was converted into sheer delight by my discovery of how to unlock my handcuffs. These handcuffs were constructed on a very simple mechanical principle. In each there was a steel pin. Pivoting on the pin were two metal gyves. One of them had a serrated edge; this locked into the other one, which was hollow, and contained a spring-and-ratchet mechanism in a deep, narrow slot.

The first gyve was shaped like a hook, the second resembled a door-latch. If you squeezed them, the ratchet operated and the handcuff became tighter. To release it required a key which pressed down on the spring and disengaged the ratchet.

When the serrated gyve was in position, there still remained a fractional amount of play in the slot. If you could slide a needle or fine wire through this gap, it was possible to press back the spring without a key. With a fair amount of pressure the two gyves could be freed.

When I at last got the handcuffs off, I was so elated that anyone seeing me at that moment would have thought I was mad. I waved my arms about, flexed them, jerked them up and down; gradually my stiff and swollen joints came back to life.

At once I tapped out the good news to my neighbour.

"I've done it!"

"What?"

"Got my handcuffs off."

"Are you getting meals now?"

"Yes. First one today."

"Mind you put handcuffs back meal-times."

"Right."

"Good night."

I remained in a triumphant mood for the rest of the day. I had scored a notable victory; I felt I had actually regained part of my freedom. When I heard the iron door creak open at the end of the afternoon, I put the handcuffs back again. Then I sat waiting for my mess-tin of soup. This time it was accompanied by a hunk of bread and a little margarine. I pushed the tin I had emptied that morning out into the corridor. When everyone was served and the guards had gone, I freed my hands once more and sat down to enjoy my meal.

The most unpleasant moment in the routine of prison life is when you wake up. It always took me some time—especially after the fantastic dreams I often had—to return to the grim realities of my situation. Then, as soon as the day's activities were well under way, I lapsed into a state of chronic boredom.

That was why I used to climb up to the fanlight as soon as it was safe. It passed the time and gave me something to do. Now my hands were free it was easy to get up there; I no longer needed the bedstead. At the least noise I would jump down again and sit on the bed, in the normal way.

I spent more and more time in this way. Soon, apart from meal-times and my visits to the wash-house, I was up there continually. Each morning I used to talk to Bury; during the afternoons I would stare for hours at the walls and courtyard. Sometimes I caught a glimpse of the women going down to wash at the far end. I felt far better organised now. Every day I scratched a fresh line on my wall-calendar; and as the number of lines grew, I thought: Time goes by and you are still there. Why not escape?

Food, and my snatched moments with Bury—and my contact through him with the outside world—gave me fresh zest for life. I showed him my unshackled hands.

"Look!" I said.

"How did you do it?"

"With your safety-pin."

"Careful. You might be seen."

I asked him about my letters.

"Everything's under control."

Every week a letter was smuggled out of the prison; into it I poured all my anxieties and fears. Here is what I wrote on April 30:

My Dearest Mother,

I am imprisoned here for an indefinite period. For the moment I am, you might say, resident in Lyons. I have done my duty to the best of my ability. I want this letter to be sent on to my wife's address, so that she can read it when she gets back, if I'm not there by then. Now that I can no longer act as a soldier, I think continually of her and of my children. If she had been there, she

*would never have let me volunteer for such duties because of the
children; but she must have realised that I was only doing what
I had to do, and she has always known that my loyalty to my
country had to take precedence over everything else . . .*

I had said good-bye to my wife and my elder son Serge at Port
Lyautey. Christian was born after my departure on November 8,
1942, the day the Americans landed. My daughter Chantal had
been too small to make the journey with my wife when she joined
me in Morocco; she had stayed with her grandmother.

*. . . I would like my sons to go to Saint-Cyr and become officers.
You are all in my thoughts; you have never been closer to me
than you are now. I feel isolated, dreadfully cut off; but I regret
nothing. What I did was done for my country. I ran no greater
risks than those who are fighting on the Tunisian front; if I had
stayed in North Africa I should have been with them now.*

*I want to close on a note of confidence and hope. Things are
going well; I have always had a lucky star. I shall come back.*

I had a double purpose in writing: to prevent my family being
scared, and to let them know (though strictly I should not have
done) why I was in prison. I also wanted to pass on some personal
requests in case I failed to survive.

To mitigate the fear which such a letter might provoke, I
added:

*There is a woman in the cell next to mine. She is undergoing
the same deprivations as I am.*

In fact, throughout the previous night she had been shut
in the latrines opposite my cell, without either mattress or blankets.
The figures chalked on the latrine door showed that she was
to go without food for three days.

Her name was Gilberte Champion, and she was a wireless-
operator for the Resistance. She had been arrested while transmitting a message. This mother of three children taught me such
a lesson in courage that I forgot my own troubles. I was only
three yards from her; but I could give her no help.

That night there was a tremendous noise in the corridor. I sprang to the spy-hole. Fränzel and two civilian warders had come for her. A moment later shriek after horrible shriek rang through the still night air. There was nothing I could do. I held my breath and listened. After a while they brought her back to the latrine and shut her in. I heard her sobbing. When they had gone I called her softly through the spy-hole.

"Can you hear me?"

"Yes." Her voice was faint and weak.

"Did they—"

"Yes."

"Don't despair. Tomorrow you'll get something to eat. And they'll have to give you a cell."

I could not sleep any more that night. I lay awake till dawn, bitter and miserable, thinking.

May 14.

At the sound of footsteps in the corridor I jumped down from the fanlight, sat on my bed, refastened the handcuffs and waited apprehensively. The key turned in my lock, and the door was opened by an N.C.O., who put a parcel down at my feet without saying a word. I saw Fränzel watching behind him. Then they both went away, and I heard the central door slam loudly.

A parcel, a real parcel addressed to me, with my name and cell number on it. I turned it over and examined it carefully. Then, without undue hurry, I opened it and examined its contents. It had already been searched, but nothing, I thought, had actually been removed. I found two shirts, two pairs of drawers, two pairs of socks, two washing flannels, two handkerchiefs, some toilet soap and a packet of razor blades. It all smelt of home, of my family; it symbolised freedom for me.

Deeply moved, I spent a long time handling these simple objects, absorbing the atmosphere of the outside world from contact with them. Then, with the most meticulous care, I put them away.

My neighbour, somewhat disturbed at this unexpected visit, tapped on the wall to find out what had happened. But I could not bring myself to tell him; he could not share my good fortune, and the news would only increase his own wretchedness.

"Bury," I called out softly, "are you there?"
He answered at once.
I said, "I've been sent a parcel of clothes."
"Good. Someone knows you're here."
"I have a letter for you."
"Fine. Throw it down."
"No, look: I've got a better way."

I had fastened the four corners of my handkerchief together into a small bag, and tied this to the end of the string which had held my parcel together. I lowered it through the window. Bury took the letter. He said: "Tomorrow I'll get you something extra to eat." Then he went back to join Blanchonnet and Kuster, who were strolling round the sunlit courtyard.

Thus the days passed by; and every morning the row of lines on the wall grew longer.

Blasts on the whistle and voices in the corridor; black *ersatz* coffee a little later; a wash at mid-morning, hours spent gazing through the fanlight; dinner; then wall-tapping till it was time to sleep. The routine became fixed and immutable.

One evening my neighbour asked me if I knew the Penal Battalion Song. I said I remembered one verse and the chorus. After that, for hours at a time, I occupied myself with humming a tune I had known long ago, trying to recall the words. As they came back to me I tapped them out on the wall.

Why, I wondered, had he asked me about this particular song? Where had he heard it? Probably in Saint-Paul prison; some fellow-prisoner, formerly in the Bataillon d'Afrique, must have taught it to him. Both words and tune carried an atmosphere of fatalistic resignation. They put me into a melancholy mood, and I could not get them out of my mind for days.

March on, said the song, *march on.* It was a hard, endless march, and there was no falling out, we had to grit our teeth and get on with it, sniped at continually by boredom, misery, hunger and idleness.

About the end of May there was an unusual stir in the corridor after the morning ration of coffee had been served out. Rapid footsteps approached my cell.

My former escort, the S.S. sergeant, stamped in, checked my handcuffs, and ordered me to get out of the cell.

He shoved me into the corridor and took me down to the courtyard. The clean morning air and the sense of freedom from confinement gave me a strange and delightful sensation. I had little time to enjoy it, however. There was a black Citroën drawn up between the walls, and I was at once hustled into it. The S.S. man sat down beside me, pistol in hand. The doors of the car were locked. There was no chance to repeat my earlier escapade, especially since the German (who had no more forgotten it than I had) never took his eyes off me. Occasionally he muttered unpleasant threats at me in his own language.

Beyond the railway bridge the car swung round to the left, and sped past the river wharves in the direction of Perrache station. Now we were passing along an avenue of trees; the leaves had grown, thick and green, since I last came this way in April. The changed colour of the landscape, the warm air, even the appearance of those passers-by I glimpsed, all offered a picture of late spring. I felt like a wild beast let out of its cage. I had so little time to absorb these precious details, and the effect they had on me was so strong, that I almost forgot my angry escort and the ordeal which awaited me. I only came back to reality when the car swung into the drive of the Station Hotel. It pulled up sharply in front of the entrance.

The driver got out and unlocked the rear door. My S.S. escort guided me into the lobby, and so to the lift.

For a brief moment I saw a man's face reflected in the mirror —a thick, black, bloodstained beard, long, tangled hair, pallid complexion, hollow eyes. I could not restrain a gasp of horror when I realised I was looking at myself.

We walked a little way down a corridor where a soldier sat on guard at a table. Then my escort, still covering me with his revolver, pushed me into a room which I remembered only too well. It had obviously once been a lounge; now the furniture had all been cleared out, and it was used as a waiting-room.

About a dozen people were sitting there in silence, while a sentry armed with a machine-pistol watched over them. They were probably prisoners from Montluc who had been brought here by truck. Automatically I moved towards a chair, with the intention of sitting down; but the S.S. man seized me with some violence, pushed me into a corner, and with vigorous imprecations conveyed to me that I must stand there, with my face to the wall.

Clearly I was going to be interrogated again.

Whatever happens, I thought, I must stick it out. The organisation has been warned now, and all necessary precautions have been taken. But if I alter my story at all, I shall let myself in for endless questioning, probably fresh torture, simply because they'll think I know a lot more than I've told them.

I had to deny everything, even in the face of evidence; I must not admit having been involved.

Hour after hour I stood in my corner, staring at the flowered wall-paper. Occasionally it blurred and danced in front of my eyes. All the time I was strengthening myself to carry out my resolution. As I became more tired it grew into an obsession, deep-rooted and immovable.

"Why did you try to escape?" Timann asked me. His cold, sharp eyes stared into mine.

"I was brought up in the mountains. I can't stand prison life."

"Fair enough. In your place I should have done the same. But now you're going to give me your word not to try again."

"How could I escape? You know the prison as well as I do. What use would such a promise be?"

"Very well," he said, disregarding my remarks. "We shall see each other again soon."

Thereupon he took me back to the waiting-room. Flabbergasted, I retreated to my corner again.

What was he after? No beating-up; not even a slapped face. Why this changed attitude? Was he too busy to give me the full treatment?

Behind me I heard the comings and goings of prisoners under escort; occasionally a German walked from one office to another. Timann had behaved with such scrupulous correctness that—bearing in mind his technique during previous interviews—I completely failed to understand his motives. Was it a psychological trick? Perhaps he was going to call me back unexpectedly. Then it would be a different story.

From time to time I half-turned my head and caught a brief glimpse of my fellow-prisoners. Their long beards, exhausted expressions and ragged clothes all reflected the extreme physical and mental suffering they had undergone.

Perhaps, I thought, they are accused of more serious crimes than I am. Perhaps their lot is worse than mine. Things aren't going too badly for me. If I hadn't tried to escape, I should be sitting where they are, un-handcuffed, and very sensible too. Is it not better to copy them, and learn an inexhaustible patience?

There was an exclamation behind me. I turned round and saw a tall young man struggling in the grip of two civilian guards.

"I'm a Frenchman!" he exclaimed, over and over again, in a loud voice.

"You come from Strasbourg. You're not French. You're German."

"I'm a Frenchman," he repeated, "a Frenchman, I tell you!"

This interrogation went on for a while in the waiting-room. Poor devil, I thought; he's got guts. Then he was taken outside, and I heard him being beaten. But throughout he kept repeating the same words.

I was wrong: his was the better way. To hell with patience and resignation. I would, I must escape, and at the first opportunity.

The hours passed slowly. I was exhausted and hungry. Late in the afternoon, my S.S. guard stormed into the room. I did not move. He got hold of me and dragged me towards the other prisoners, who had got to their feet and were forming up two by two. He handcuffed them in pairs, right to left hand—a useless precaution as far as I was concerned, since I was permanently handcuffed anyway. Then we all went down the passage, descended the stairs, and marched to the waiting truck.

But when I tried to get in, the S.S. sergeant stopped me.

I returned to Montluc in the car which had brought me that morning, but by a different route. We passed a good many people in the streets, and I could not help resenting their apparent indifference. How could they live a normal peaceful life while hundreds of fellow human beings were being tortured by the enemy in their own town?

In the courtyard I indicated by signs that I was hungry, and returned to my cell carrying a spoon and mess-tin. I was glad to get back to my own private corner and the life I had created there; even to solitude, with only my bed for company.

My neighbour tapped out a question on the wall.

"Interrogation?"

"Yes. About my escape."

"All right?"

"Yes."

"Good night."

"Good night."

3

The following morning Fränzel came into my cell and told me to pack. It was June 2. I barely had time to scramble down from the fanlight and replace my handcuffs. I hardly wore them at all now except at meal-times and when I went out to wash.

"Come on, pack. Be quick about it."

To leave this cell affected me more than I would have supposed; it considerably increased the apprehension I felt at such a sudden summons. I had grown used to it; Bury, the condemned man in the next cell, all the little habits I had developed were now an accepted part of my life. At this moment, if I had had the choice, I would gladly have stayed where I was.

I put my few possessions into the cardboard box which had come with the clothes I had been sent. Fränzel stood waiting impatiently at the door. He swung his leather truncheon to and fro threateningly. I was as quick as I could be—though I would dearly have loved to tap out a farewell on the cell wall.

In the corridor a bare-headed orderly was collecting the mess-tins.

I turned to go in the direction of the courtyard. Fränzel stopped me.

"No," he said, "this way."

39

I walked in front of him up the staircase. On the second floor we turned to the left. He stopped me and took off my handcuffs. Then the door of cell number 107, the last but one on the right, shut behind me.

All the cells in Montluc Prison are the same. Sometimes the concrete ledge which does duty for a table is differently placed; it may be in the corner below the fanlight, or on the opposite side above the earth-closet. When it is under the fanlight it gives one the inestimable advantage of a foothold to climb up by. The cells are about two yards wide and three deep; their height I should guess to be something approaching ten feet.

They have four openings. In the outer wall, near the ceiling, there is a narrow rectangular window. This is protected by a grill of seven vertical and two horizontal bars; there is also the fanlight. In the opposite wall, by the door, is a niche for the light-bulb. This is furnished with a little door made of ground glass, surrounded by a stout steel frame, which can be opened and shut by the occupant. Underneath, at floor level, is a cubby-hole designed to take the prisoner's pail. It has a solid metal door with an enormous bolt. If you explore this cubby-hole, you will discover the mouth of a narrow chimney or air-hole, where things can be hidden if necessary. The door itself is made of reinforced oak. It contains two panels, each comprising six thick boards, and is held in an equally thick frame. From the inside these planks present a smooth surface; there are rivet-heads visible in the frame, and the small spy-hole in the top panel, and that is all. Outside it is a different matter. Iron clamps are riveted across each corner to strengthen the boards; and half-way up the door there is a huge bolt, made of steel and brass, with a heavy lock above it.

The tiny size of the cell somehow makes all these complicated bolts and bars more alarming. Your being is at once permeated and corrupted by the filthy greyish walls, by the smell of mildew, bed-bugs and urine.

Your furniture is reduced to a basic minimum. There is a

wooden bedstead strung with wire; a mattress; a ticky bolster which matches the walls; two blankets; a latrine-pail; and, in one corner, a primitive broom. The cell doors open outwards on to a gallery which runs round the whole building, and is served by a single central staircase.

The main prison block is rectangular in shape, and consists of two floors. Round the flat roof runs a parapet, outside which is a yard-wide cat-walk, with a sheer drop beneath it. Along the roof runs a glass penthouse, which contains a number of windows. These can be opened from below by a system of rods and levers. Through them a little light filters down into the galleries, and the building gets a certain amount of fresh air.

The two outer walls are about twenty-five feet high, and roughly ten yards apart; the space between is continually patrolled by guards. These walls are quite smooth except at the top, where there is a sloping gutter to carry rainwater outside the perimeter.

The inner enclosure is connected with the central block by four walls of medium height. These quarter the grounds into four communicating courtyards, and house several smaller buildings. The largest one, opening on the main gate, contains the police post, the kitchens, the blacksmith's shop and the infirmary. The second is reserved for prisoners to take exercise in. Here there are a wash-house, a workshop (at the time converted into a recreation-room), and a wooden barracks occupied by Jewish prisoners. The windows of the women's dining-hall open on to the third court, and those of the infirmary on to another smaller yard. At the end of this yard runs a covered gallery; its tiled roof is just about level with the inner wall.

There is a small iron wicket by which one can pass straight through to the courthouse. The buildings set aside for the administration of military justice lie immediately beyond the outer wall, outside the prison perimeter and backing on to the railway-line. Nevertheless, they form part of the building; they are surrounded by a fairly high wall which is linked to the main enclosure. If you stand on the railway-bridge, a little way off, you can see the courthouse in the foreground, and behind it, just visible between the two walls, the top story of the main block, its front dotted with barred windows. If you follow the road past the court-room, you reach a large square at the lower end, which is kept out of bounds to the public. Here you can see the ancient fortress of Montluc, and on the right the entrance to the military prison. It is an impressive sight, but not one to be lingered over.

The whole of Montluc is grey: a dark, dirty grey, which spreads over the whitewashed walls and reduces them to the same colour as the cobbled courtyards and the cracked paint which is daubed over the corridors and cells. The grey-green uniform worn by the warders harmonises perfectly with this depressing *décor*.

The warders were all drawn from a regiment of the German Army stationed in Lyons. Some of them must have seen active service: they wore a combat badge, or a large gaudy medal ribbon sewn slantwise above the second button of their tunics. When they were on guard-duty they wore a steel helmet, and carried American tommy-guns with the safety-catch released, not to mention a bayonet. Their boots, I could not help noticing, were always polished to perfection, their belts and buttons shining, their equipment in perfect order. Fränzel saw to this; he was a senior warrant officer. In civilian life he had been a circus ringmaster; now he was chief warder of a prison. He certainly took his job seriously. He always carried a short thick blackjack, which was attached to his wrist by a lanyard, and his loud voice could be heard bawling all day in every corner of the compound. His second-in-command, a company sergeant-major, was a very different character, who seemed out of place in such a setting. He obviously disliked the unpleasant duties he had to perform. He was an attractive, even an impressive figure, and made an odd contrast with his immediate superior. You could tell when he was on duty by the general atmosphere of peacefulness.

During the day two sentries were on duty: one at the main gate, the other patrolling the perimeter. The system was changed as the number of prisoners increased. When I was in cell 45, at the beginning of my detention, there were only two sentries during the night as well. It was not till July, when the old workshop and the wooden barracks began to fill up, that extra precautions were taken. Every night, in cell 107, I heard the guard being mounted. If I climbed up to the fanlight I could see a sentry in the men's courtyard, near the wash-house, and guess at the presence of yet another from the regular footsteps that paced between the main staircase and the Jews' quarters.

The sergeant-major and the orderly sergeant slept on the first floor of the main block, the duty corporal in a bunk near the front entrance. Every door was locked at night. This was such a thorough business that if the Gestapo brought in a prisoner at night (which they seldom did) they not only had to ring at the outer gate, but get through a whole series of obstacles: the inner wall, the guard-room, the courtyard. Finally they had to ring yet again outside the prisoners' block, and be admitted by the corporal.

The building was lit inside by a single dim lamp on the ground floor, near the staircase; this had to serve all the galleries. In each courtyard there were a few electric bulbs, but they gave little illumination.

In the perimeter, above the circular beat patrolled by the sentries, were six shaded lights, three to each wall. They were set high upon the inner bailey, a little below the guttering.

I laid out my possessions on the bracket and then sat down, head in hands, to consider my changed situation. I had been taken out of the condemned block and my handcuffs had been removed. My case seemed to be taking a turn for the better; it was even possible that my abortive escape was to be forgotten. Almost certainly I was now to lead a communal life, and have the privileges of reasonable exercise and a better diet. I would make new friends, too; but no one could take Bury's place, or match the warm sympathy he had shown me at moments of crisis. I should miss his reassuring presence each day in the courtyard, his sympathy and encouragement. Worst of all, I had lost in him my only means of communication with my family and friends; I was again cut off from the outside world.

It was late before I fell asleep, depressed and exhausted, still thinking of Bury.

I woke from a heavy sleep just as the coffee ration was being served out. I went to my door for the inevitable mess-tin, and swallowed the weak, luke-warm liquid at one gulp. The noise and bustle up here contrasted strongly with the quiet life I had got used to on the ground floor: rattling keys, buckets scraping over the concrete floor, beds being shifted, shouting voices. This unfamiliar Babel of noise reminded me that this was my first day in my new quarters.

I swept the floor and re-arranged my miserable belongings, taking care to hide such precious objects as my razor-blades and pencils. Bury was no longer available to get me fresh supplies: I should have to be more economical.

A few moments later my door was flung wide open by the duty N.C.O. Watching the preparations being made by the prisoner in the opposite cell, I realised that this must be the time for exercise. I put my empty mess-tin outside, took my bucket in one hand and my towel in the other, and stood waiting in the gallery, beside my cell door. There were more than a dozen of us on the landing. We stared at each other in silence, waiting for orders.

They came soon enough.

"At six paces interval—quick *march!* No talking!"

We filed down the stairs, a steel-helmeted soldier bringing up the rear, and went out of the main entrance behind the prisoners from the first floor. We began to move in an extended circle round the large courtyard. There we were obliged to empty our buckets in turn down an open drain, and swill a little water into them as we passed a tap outside the kitchens. Next some chlorate of lime, scooped up from a big tub, was dropped in to disinfect them; finally we left them in a long row in front of the prison building. We had to go right round the court in order to perform each part of this operation, and carefully keep our prescribed distance. Not a moment passed without one or other of our guards reminding us of this, with a hoarse "*Distanz*—six paces!"

Our column, a guard at its head, marched round the corner of the block and entered the second courtyard. It was plain our job there was to wash; without even waiting for orders, the first six prisoners made for the ablutions, while the rest started trudging round in a circle again. One guard stood near them, while another stationed himself on the other side, in front of the men's dining-hall.

All the time I was on the look-out for a face or gait I knew. Round we went, slowly; occasionally one of us paused (generally opposite the guard) to regulate his distance from the man in front.

It was fascinating to study these prisoners. They were drawn from many strata of society, yet all had their new anonymous status in common. However widely they might differ in age, profession, social rank, income, education or beliefs, they were nevertheless united by the common ideal which they served, and which, through the suffering it involved, made them all equal.

There were exceptions, of course: especially Martin, who was there for black-market dealings. Besides, one look at him was enough. That fat red face, those eyes sheltering nervously behind tortoise-shell glasses, that heavy, clumsy gait, the querulous self-pity which oozed from him—all this discouraged anyone from confiding in him, or even giving him a sympathetic glance. But the rest were different—Nathan, Julian, Grimaud, Aymard, de Pury, Duflot, Schoeller. They were there because in their own fashion, with or without success, but with fierce determination, they had continued the struggle against the enemy. The crimes with which they were charged were such things as gun-running, espionage, sabotage, subversive propaganda, liaison with the enemy, and organising intelligence or Resistance groups.

Round the court we went; our dismal procession skirted the wooden barracks, passed beneath the windows of the dining-hall, moved on towards the workshop, and completed its circuit near the ablutions. Here, every ten minutes, at a sign from the German guard, six prisoners jumped forward to take the places of their predecessors, while the latter returned to the ranks.

My turn came at last. I washed myself slowly, watching my companions. Next to me a huge fellow had, without a trace of modesty, stripped himself stark naked and was splashing about under the tap. The water chuckled over the cement floor; several of us quickly washed out a handkerchief or a pair of drawers. At the far end I noticed two friends surreptitiously whispering to each other.

When we had all finished, the circular promenade still went on for a little longer. I took advantage of this to fill my lungs with fresh air, and drink in the blueness of the sky. I even (as far as I remember) managed to do some arm and leg exercises, to tone up my muscles. My neighbour of the wash-house watched this performance with some curiosity, and the guards with blank indifference.

Fränzel, standing on the staircase, shouted out to us to stop. We each picked up our bucket and filed through the passage to the stairs. The column divided into two on the first floor, and we all went back to our cells.

The man opposite me—he looked about thirty—stared hard at me before closing his door. Then I shut my own, and a moment later heard the key turn in the lock.

What was I going to do now I could no longer climb up to the fanlight and see my friend Bury? I could not even tap out messages on the wall. Once more I was alone, alone with time, with those tyrannous minutes and hours I should have to kill one after the other. I felt I should have to struggle hard if I was not to lose, little by little, the strength and hope which the miracle of Bury's intervention had sparked off in me.

I chose a clean, smooth patch of wall and started my calendar again in pencil. The tally was growing impressively long. Where would it stop? How long would I remain here?

The next few days I bore my lot calmly, keeping a prudent reserve with those who tried to talk to me in the wash-house. Nevertheless, one of them attracted my interest more than the rest. His cell was on the first floor. He was a tall, muscular young man, and gave an unusual impression of energy.

"Where are you from?" he asked me one day.

"Haute-Savoie. What about you?"

"Marseilles. What's your job?"

"I'm an Army officer."

When the German guard turned away from our corner, the man from Marseilles said: "Follow me to the latrines. We must talk a little more."

When our batch left the wash-house, he raised his hand and, at a nod from the guard, went over to the double latrines. They stood against the wall of the courtyard. A moment later I did the same. I squatted down on the free seat next to his, taking care, as he had done, to hang my towel on the door. This showed that the closet was occupied.

"How long have you been here?" he asked quietly.

"Since April 18."

"I've been here a fortnight, but this is the first time I've seen you. Where have you been?"

"In the condemned block."

"Why?"

"I tried to escape."

"How?"

"Jumping out of a moving car. I was caught again at once."

"Meet me here again tomorrow. We can arrange it with a little care. What's your name?"

"Devigny. What's yours?"

"Nathan."

I went back to my cell in a more cheerful mood.

You have to imagine the kind of life we were leading to understand how important this short conversation was for us. Our days were absolutely empty. After our morning exercise we waited for our mid-day soup; all we had to look forward to after that was supper. No newspapers, no books, nothing to occupy our time. Waiting: all our time was spent waiting; waiting for exercise and food, food and exercise. Message-tapping, too, was out of the question; the cells on either side of mine were empty.

Occasionally someone asked the time; less often some bold

fellow took the risk (especially during the guards' meal-times) of calling out to a friend by name, or passing on some scrap of news.

Nathan admitted to me later that he had tried to escape in exactly the same way as me. He was caught because he had hidden in the back of a shop, and the owner gave him away. The Germans had broken two of his ribs when they beat him up afterwards.

"How can I get out of here?" I asked him.

"Look at these walls above our heads, and think of the number of guards. You can't do a thing from the inside."

I agreed. "The only possible way is outside, during a transfer from one prison to another. I'm ready to have another shot at it, whatever the risk."

The guard, who must have guessed we were talking, began to shout "*Silentz! Silentz!*"

Nathan said: "Don't move. Wait a moment before you go out."

After a fortnight's daily march round the courtyard, I knew everyone by sight. Sometimes a new face appeared and joined in the wretched ritual. I could not help feeling sorry for anyone who found himself thus brutally thrust into this nightmare existence. Surprise and consternation were written all over his face. Generally the newcomer would try to talk; he would gaze terror-struck as the guard sprang at him, shook him like a plum-tree at picking-time, and swore at him in a language he could not understand.

But after a while this newcomer, like the rest, would acquire our standard appearance: tangled hair, long beard, frayed clothes, and listless walk. He would learn how to talk without being caught by the guards—not to mention the complicated stratagem by which we managed to visit the wash-house twice during the same morning, and the latrines even more frequently.

Along with Nathan, I had become a specialist at this game. No one knew better than we did how to get into the most favourable position in the queue; we went through the necessary pantomime with gusto, and displayed astonishment verging on the edge of simple-mindedness if any suspicions arose in the German guard's mind. Our trick came off almost every time, because we took the elementary precaution of performing it under the noses of soldiers carefully selected for their comparative passivity. Grimaud had found an even better method; he had set up as an amateur barber. Every day we could see him at work in the covered gallery, scraping away at the longest and toughest beards with a cut-throat razor he had somehow managed to keep. Occasionally he could exchange a word or two with his victim, who sat groaning under the strokes of a horribly blunt blade.

So, gradually, despite our guards and the six-pace rule (not to mention the system of solitary confinement) we contrived to find out each others' names, addresses, and interests. The carefully averted eye could sense a current of sympathy which might derive from a common age, home, or, perhaps, a life bound up with similar interests.

On May 30, a Sunday, I found myself at the back of the column, behind a new arrival. He stared at us one after the other with an expression in which curiosity, pity and compassion were so strongly mingled that he had the appearance of one gazing on a new and unimagined world.

I noted his well-kept clothes and intellectual bearing, and wondered what he had done to be where he was. He could hardly be a parachutist or a saboteur; perhaps he was a radio-operator or a journalist whose tongue had wagged indiscreetly. Yes, I decided, he must be a journalist. I might even know of him. I was determined to get to the bottom of the matter before the morning's exercise was over.

I edged closer to him.

"Are you a journalist?" I whispered.

"No, a Protestant minister."

"Where?"

"In Lyons."

"What is your name?"

"De Pury."

"Keep your distance there!" bellowed one of the guards. I was sorry to have been responsible for this rebuke to our new companion; but I was glad that I had satisfied my curiosity.

The next day I said to Nathan: "You see that bald chap who arrived yesterday? He's a minister."

"The other one, the tall, dark chap with a moustache, is an English parachutist," he replied.

"How do you know?"

"He told me in sign-language. He doesn't speak a word of French. When I go out I'll leave you a sheet of newspaper on the wall. Pass it on to someone else tomorrow."

"Have you thought about a plan of escape?"

"Yes, I've thought about it. Quite impossible from this place."

In this way I accustomed myself to a new routine. My body and spirit were slowly being exhausted by privations and loneliness, but I was still continually obsessed with the idea of escaping. Bury, who in some mysterious way had managed to come to my door to say good-bye, shook me out of the lethargy into which I was sinking. I had a quick exchange with him through the spy-hole.

I asked him if he was being moved.

"Yes," he said, "to Fresnes."

I said: "Thanks for everything. You saved my life. I hope we meet after the war. God bless you!"

"Good luck to you. And good-bye."

"Tell me quickly, before you go," I said. "What about my neighbour—the fellow who was next door to my old cell?"

"He was shot last week."

"Thank you," I said after a moment. "Good-bye."

He pushed some lumps of sugar and a bar of chocolate under my door and moved away silently, leaving me in great distress. I was moved almost to weeping-point.

4

Towards the end of June I made what appeared a somewhat commonplace discovery. But it changed my prison routine in the most radical way, and made demands on my patience and endurance which I could never have foreseen.

Often I used to sit facing the door on my bucket, which I would previously cover with a folded blanket. Why in this particular position? Instinctively, I suppose; it was through the door that my meals arrived, and here also that I could most clearly hear what was going on in the corridor. To occupy my mind, I moved my wall-calendar to the centre of the door. I used to stare for hours at that list of days, counting them over and over again. I broke it down analytically, making a separate column for Sundays and public holidays, and adding a special symbol for weeks.

Day after day I looked at those smooth brown oak boards without noticing anything odd about them. Then one day by chance, my eye wandering idly up and down the narrow crack between two panels, I noticed some different wood behind them, almost white. I got up and scrutinised the crack closely, making sure I was unobserved. Then I took the aluminum spoon I had managed to keep, slid its flat handle into the crack, and pressed gently. There was no doubt about it; the wood which held the

51

boards together was not oak, but some softer timber, probably deal.

The six vertical boards were held in place at the top and bottom by tenons mortised into the door-frame. Each board was thus cut into a tenon at both ends. Longitudinally, however, it was channelled with a mortise for the whole height of the door. When the boards were set in position side by side, each juxtaposed pair of mortises formed a long rectangular slot. To secure each board to its neighbour, a matching strip of wood was keyed into this slot, and formed a double tenon. It was the different colour of the wood from which these tenons had been fashioned which showed me how the door was put together.

My discovery filled me with excitement; I realised at once that the door could be taken to pieces. I had no idea how; that did not matter. I was happy again. I was going to have an occupation, an object to my existence. I could once more use my wits, my imagination, and my technical skill.

I got to work at once. I had to have a tool. The aluminum spoon had been useful enough for probing between the planks, but it was useless for the purpose I had in mind: I wanted to cut through the central tenon, from top to bottom, and aluminum was far too soft a metal to perform such a task. I would have to keep my eyes open, every meal-time, for an iron spoon. This, I thought, might serve my requirements. I could exchange it for the aluminum one, and keep it.

The end of the handle, I thought, could be given a cutting edge by sharpening it on the cement floor. The resultant tool would resemble a kind of joiner's chisel.

I got my iron spoon a few days later. Hour after hour I sat in the blind corner of the cell, by the earth-closet, grinding the flat end of the handle on each side in turn. I stopped at regular intervals to listen for footsteps, and then turned back to my regular, unwearying movement. Occasionally I would examine the spoon to see what effect I was having on it. It was a long, irksome, exhausting task; but in the end I was satisfied. The experiments I made with this amateur chisel on my bedstead seemed quite successful.

The next morning, in the wash-house, I said to Nathan: "I'm going to dismantle my cell door. It can be done."

He asked me why.

"I don't know. Something to keep me occupied."

"You're running risks for nothing. They won't let you off again."

"I don't care," I said. "I can't sit about all day doing nothing. It's driving me mad."

"*Silentz!*" bellowed one of the guards. Our short conversation was over.

When I got back to my cell, I began work at once. To get out, I calculated, I should have to remove three boards. It would not, however, be necessary to work on all of them. If I cleared one to start with I could save myself a lot of trouble. I would first have to release it from the planks on either side by chiselling through the two long strips of wood which held them together. After that there were the tenons at top and bottom to be severed. This done, I ought to be able to pull the board into the cell. The next two boards on either side could then, with a little loosening, be slid into the centre, and only their upper and lower tenons would need to be removed. In this way, with a minimum of effort, I could make an opening wide enough to get through.

To begin with, then, I had to separate the boards from each other. This was not particularly difficult in itself. All I needed to do was to slide my chisel into the crack, apply fairly hard pressure, and work it up and down. I could feel the blade bite into the wood, and then begin to cut through it. What worried me was the noise I made. I broke off from the job at frequent intervals and listened for a long time. Occasionally I coughed loudly to cover the sound of splintering; at the least suspicion of a foot-step I would abandon everything and throw myself on my bed, in a convincingly listless way.

The best time for my operation was during the guards' meal-times—that is, after the prisoners had had their soup-ration.

At regular intervals I pushed a twig from my broom under the door and, with some difficulty, collected the dust and tiny fragments of wood which accumulated outside. I went on at my project day in, day out, never hurrying, yet never stopping.

About this time the next cell, number 109, received an occupant. He arrived late in the afternoon, escorted by Fränzel, whom I recognised by the unpleasant trick he had of running his bunch of keys along the banisters as he moved. The resultant noise grated disagreeably on my nerves. I heard my new neighbour moving about for a while; then all was still. I decided it would be wiser to abandon my work till I had taken a look at him during exercise the following morning.

He was a thin, pale, stooping man—this characteristic lessened his considerable height—with long, white hair, and sad eyes deepset under shaggy brows. I saw him when the duty N.C.O. opened his door for our daily parade. He must have been sixty, perhaps more. He stood quite near me, soberly dressed, and (like the rest of us) without either belt, tie, or shoe-laces. This somehow accentuated the atmosphere of utter fatigue and lassitude which impregnated his whole personality.

I kept my eyes fixed on him so as to draw his attention at the first opportunity. He looked at me and at once averted his eyes.

"Where are you from?" I asked in a low voice.

"What business is that of yours?" he replied.

In the wash-house, a little later, I told Nathan about this.

"See that new chap—the big man in grey just going past now, the one with white hair? He's got the cell next to mine. I tried to talk to him and he snubbed me. He doesn't look very forthcoming, does he?"

"Better watch him. Did you know some of our lot were moved yesterday?"

"Where to?"

"Compiègne. I've been counting. Five missing this morning from my floor."

I said: "It'll be our turn soon. We've been here a long time now. Whatever happens, I'm going to try and make a break for it."

"So am I. I haven't the least desire to be rubbed out by these bastards."

On my way back, as I passed by the open door of cell 109, I noticed that there were no personal possessions whatsoever in it. Once more, when the guard was down the other end of the corridor, I tried to talk to my new neighbour.

"What's your name?" I asked.

The prisoner across the way looked at the new-comer and then shook his head at me. Then he closed his door. It seemed like some kind of warning.

That day my carpentering got very little further. I was worried and preoccupied: not so much by the difficulty of the work as the attitude and behaviour of my neighbour.

The next day I tried again, with equally little success.

A stool-pigeon would be only too glad to talk in such circumstances, I thought, baffled. This man is no stool-pigeon. But he is certainly hiding something; and till you've found out what it is, you'd better watch out.

Sometimes, as I had done in the condemned block, I would climb up to the fanlight and stare out at the sky. Beyond the walls I could see the tobacco factory; further to the right was the railway bridge. From time to time I saw pedestrians and vehicles moving across it, or perhaps a tram, which went grinding on along the tracks that followed the outer wall.

One evening when I had already been up on my perch for some time, I heard a most extraordinary rumpus going on in cell 109. There were loud creaks as the bedstead was shifted, and then a scrabbling at the fanlight. A moment later I became aware that my neighbour, too, was admiring the landscape. It seemed a good moment to start another conversation, especially as the courtyard was empty.

"Can you hear me?" I said. "I'm here, next door to you."

"Yes, I can hear you. Please leave me alone. If you go on pestering me with your attentions, I shall report you."

"Fair enough. I don't mean you any harm," I said, and at once climbed down, more perplexed and disturbed than ever. Then I settled myself for the night; but for a long time sleep eluded me.

Despite this irritating incident, and the vague threat which it implied, I went on methodically with the dismantling of my cell door during the next few days. At the same time I redoubled my precautions. Eventually, as I had intended, three of the boards were completely separated for the whole of their length. There was, however, no question of now turning my attention to the tenons at top and bottom. They were, it transpired, made of oak, not deal; it would have been a tough job with a real cold chisel, let alone my improvised tool. The spoon-handle would have had no effect on such hard wood. I decided that my only hope lay in tackling the door-frame itself.

There were two possible lines of approach. I could either cut into the wood of the lintel till the tenon was completely freed, or else dispense with detailed measurements and remove an entire section of the door-frame from above the three planks. The second method seemed, on the whole, preferable, and I set about it at once. The piece I took out could be replaced (though I had yet to find a way of keeping it in position) and would be easy enough to camouflage. Another important factor governing my decision was that the grain of the oak, in the area which concerned me, ran exactly right; even with my clumsy chisel I could make the two vertical incisions I required. I would not need to perform the same operation at the bottom; a little ordinary chiselling would bevel the edge of the door-sill, and then the boards, already three-quarters free, could be levered forward.

I had to get hold of a second spoon. To exert sufficient pressure to force the cut piece out required the insertion of at least two levers in the narrow space between the lintel and the upper part of the door. Again I managed to keep a spoon after one meal, and I made a preliminary experiment which gave me considerable satisfaction. An extra hard effort would almost certainly do the trick.

I had to cover the noise I was bound to make. To help do this I put the bucket handy by one foot. After our midday meal, when the Germans were resting, I inserted the two spoon-handles and levered at the wood; gently at first, and then with a sharp pressure. The oak groaned and creaked; then, suddenly, there was a frightful crack and a piece of wood over a foot long flew out into the cell. Just as it broke loose I exploded in a violent fit of coughing, and kicked the bucket over on the concrete floor.

There was absolute silence. A spoon in each hand, I stood motionless in front of the door, nervously examining the horrible mess I had made. I was breathless with apprehension. Nothing had happened outside; but I observed that the occupant of the cell across the way had his eye glued to the spy-hole, and clearly intended to stay there.

I could not afford to waste time; there was a complicated piece of camouflage to be done. I put the section of wood back in its place and tried to find some way of making it stay there. The break was not a clean one; both the lintel and the section I had removed bore traces of splintering. The loose piece held well enough when I pushed it back into position, but I could not risk its falling at the least shock—if the door was slammed, for example. Moreover, if I wanted to carry my work a stage further, I had to be able to take this key-piece out and replace it without difficulty.

I had the whole afternoon before me. I carefully scrutinised the gaping scar in the middle of the door-frame. By the evening I was in a position to stand back and admire my finished handiwork. I was completely satisfied with it.

With the help of a razor-blade I whittled a little wedge, shaped more or less like a tenon, and fixed it on the bottom right-hand side of the removable piece. (The break at this end was somewhat slanting and irregular, which helped me.) Then I carved a corresponding mortise-like hole in the lintel itself, and cut away the worst of the splinters to form a flush surface. The loose wood was now inserted in its place; it pivoted out on this home-made hinge like a shutter. I pressed it back and further secured it with two tiny flat wedges inserted between the lintel itself and the top edge of the frame. This kept it firm, but not inconveniently so. When I had shaved away all the splinters I chewed some paper into a pap, rubbed it on the floor to blacken it, and puttied it into the cracks that still remained. Then, with my pencil, I disguised the joins I had made still further. Fortunately the wood was stained an extremely dark brown.

From this day on, inmates and guards alike could see (if they were interested) a towel hung carelessly up to dry over my door during morning exercise. I always seemed to have a towel that needed drying then.

Every day the column straggled round the courtyard, our movements governed by the same slow, miserable rhythm. My solitary neighbour was among them, indifferent to his surroundings, oblivious of the advances made to him, more lonely even than we were. I watched him all the time, intrigued by his attitude and obsessed by the desire to pierce through the veil of mystery behind which he hid.

One morning two prisoners broke ranks to help someone who had just collapsed. The guard came up, shouting, telling them to leave him alone. The man raised himself on his knees, struggled to his feet with a great effort, picked up his hat and staggered on with the rest of us. It was my next-door neighbour.

When we went back to our cells I said to him as I passed:

"Be at your fanlight this evening."

All day this incident plagued me. He is suffering, I thought; he is suffering more than the rest of us. He must be afflicted with some ghastly disease which he is determined to conceal. I was wrong to suspect him; I should be trying to do what I can to help. As I thought this, I saw in my mind's eye his expressionless, unapproachable face.

Late that evening I climbed up to the fanlight and waited; waited for a long time, and finally knocked on the wall several times to indicate that I was there.

Soon afterwards I heard him moving his bed into place, and presently I heard him clamber up beside me.

"Are you there?" I asked. "You needn't be afraid to talk. They're all down there, round the other side."

"I am here."

"What's the matter? You're ill, and you don't tell anyone!"

"Why should I?"

"We stick together in here. We share each others' troubles."

"I'm not suffering," he said. "It's all one to me."

"Have you no family?"

"No. I'm the only one left."

"No friends?"

"None."

"Did you serve in the army? What happened to you when war was declared?"

"I was unfit."

"Have you a job?"

"My factory was shut down last year."

I asked him why he was in Montluc. He said: "I was caught with some dollar notes."

I said, surprised: "Were they yours?"

"No. I got them from some Jewess I had never seen before. She passed them on to me the same day as she was arrested."

"How did they find out about you?"

"They got hold of a letter—it was in a bundle of dirty laundry . . ."

"I see. I'm sorry. What appalling luck."

He said: "Don't waste your sympathy on me. It makes no odds to me where I am, here or anywhere else."

No family, no friends, no job, no ideals: even some kind of satisfaction in *this* wretched half-life! His existence was an absolute empty void; there was no room in it for love or friendship, even for the hatred which we all shared. Such a life seemed to me wretched beyond belief.

"I understand," I said. "Nevertheless, in this place we all share the same obligations. Family, friends, work, the whole of our past—these things don't count any more. We've got to fight as long as *they* are there—against them, and with our friends."

"Fight for what, and how?"

"It would take too long to explain that up here. Even without a family or possessions, whether you like it or not, each of us has something to fight for. Refuse to admit defeat, and you have already won a victory of a sort. Without that, one might as well commit suicide."

He said: "I tried to do that. I failed."

"*What?*"

"Yes, I mean it. I tried to hang myself. You made a noise in your cell, and somehow that stopped me."

"A fine idea. I can just hear the Germans talking about it. 'Look at these Frenchmen. No guts. A little discomfort, and they kill themselves.' If you had taken that way out and left us here, you would have been no better than a deserter."

"What difference does one man more or less make?"

I said: "One man's example can infect all the rest. By to-morrow the whole prison would have known about it. The Germans would have had us at a disadvantage. We wouldn't have dared to stand up to them any longer as we do now. Dignity and courage are weapons. We can still use them, whatever our plight."

"Can a man of my age and condition go on fighting? I have become a useless burden. Why go on living when there is nothing to keep you anchored to life?"

"You are wrong," I said. "Down there in the courtyard you have seen old men as well as young ones. They are there because they fought. They are fighting still—against hunger, loneliness and boredom. They still have hope."

"Hope? What hope? Of seeing their homes and families again—"

"Not only that. They want to live. Life is our most precious possession; we do not have the right to throw it away. There is a prisoner on the first floor who has lost both arms and one eye. His loss is greater than ours. Those of us who are less handicapped than he is cannot do less than follow the splendid example he sets us."

"I have seen the man," he said, "but I never took much notice of him."

"And the woman they left to die of hunger, shut up in the

latrines opposite my old cell—she fought every inch of the way without complaint, too. She showed us how we should behave."

"You were in another cell?" he said, after a pause.

"Yes. At first I was in number 45, in the condemned block."

"You were actually condemned to death?"

"No. But it was as if I had been. I stayed down there, in handcuffs, for more than a month. I thought I was going to be shot. Then they moved me up here. I don't know why."

He said: "You must have done something serious."

"I tried to escape."

"From here?"

"No. Outside."

He said, in a wondering voice: "You wanted to get away as much as that?"

"Yes, and I still want to, more than ever. The first opportunity I get, I'm ready to take any risk to free myself. I want to die in pleasant surroundings."

He asked me then what I did, and my name. I told him.

He said: "My name is Jeantet. Eugene Jeantet."

I glanced round. "We've been talking a long time," I said. "We ought to go down now. I'm glad we had this chat. Think about what has been said. You need me as much as I need you. In this kind of misfortune you've got to keep pushing. You can never afford to give up."

There was a short silence. Then he said: "These last few days I've been watching you all the time—spying on you, if you like. I heard every noise you made in your cell, even. I wanted to feel you near me, to have something to hang on to. My life was collapsing. There was emptiness everywhere. Only you offered me a chance. Yesterday, without knowing it, you saved my life."

"I am glad," I said. "We must get down now. We can't stay here."

"Good night."

I heard him moving about at frequent intervals all through the night. I could no more sleep than he could. How could anyone sleep beside so wretched and hopeless a creature—especially when, for different reasons, he too was so close to death? While he sought it out, I fought it fiercely, not through fear of death itself, but because of my refusal to admit defeat. Had my arguments convinced him? Had I been persuasive enough? What sort of mood would I find him in the following day? Apprehensive and uneasy, I lay waiting for the dawn.

As soon as the door was opened, I looked closely at him, waiting in agony for the moment when he would turn his head in my direction. He never even glanced at me.

"Good morning," I said.

"Good morning," he replied, after a moment which seemed an age. I saw a faint flush creep into his yellow cheeks.

"For you," I said, and, picking a moment when the guard had his back to me, slipped some lumps of sugar and a piece of chocolate into his pocket.

He was obviously ashamed of his confession; I must at all costs avoid giving him the impression that I was worried by it. That was why, during the morning exercise, I behaved as if nothing had happened; but I knew that he was frequently looking in my direction. It would have been as unwise to hurry things as it would have been to appear too completely indifferent. I glanced at him occasionally to remind him of my presence.

"If you want to talk to me," I told him as we returned to the cells, "knock on my wall. Don't hesitate when you feel like it."

A little later the duty N.C.O. came by, locking each door as he went. I waited till he had gone, and then got on with my work.

The board was not, in fact, completely free yet. The door-frame had been breached, true; but this was not in itself enough. I still had to remove the wood still remaining between my "shutter" and the upper tenon in order to finish the job. So I took the "shutter" out and got to work again, cutting, filing, scraping, my ears cocked for danger the whole time, my brush within easy reach to clean up the floor at regular intervals.

The whole corridor must have got tired of the prisoner who

had caught such an abominable cold: I kept on coughing loudly to disguise the noise I was making.

Little by little the oak was chipped away round the tenon. Finally the job was done. The bottom of the door took far less time and trouble; and all I had to do was to bevel the edge of the sill opposite the central board, which would be the first to come out.

At the same time I did all I could to perfect and simplify my methods of camouflage.

Jeantet had given no signs of life. I put down his silence to shyness. Then, elated by my private success, I knocked on the wall to call him up to the fanlight. I went up myself, and after a few moments he joined me. We picked up our conversation where we had left it two days before.

"Well, Eugene," I said, "have you thought about what I told you? Isn't there something better to do than think about suicide?"

"Oh yes, I've thought about it. But what you think worthwhile means nothing to me. You have a family waiting for you outside, you're young, you want revenge. I've got nothing like that. I'm not even in good health. What have I got to look forward to? Nothing. What would I do with my freedom if I had it? I haven't the faintest idea."

"Don't say that. Here your private existence is unimportant. To the Germans you are not Eugene Jeantet, but simply an enemy through your French birth."

"What must I do, then?"

"Your duty. There are two frightful dangers which threaten all of us the whole time: despair and routine. Together they can prove fatal. We have to struggle continually to hold out against them. If we gave in, our courage, will-power and strength would be slowly sapped. All the guts would go out of us."

He said, perplexed: "How do you keep this struggle up?"

"By keeping our time full and our minds occupied. Take my own case. I've been struggling with my door for days, and now I've won."

"I don't understand."

"I have dismantled my door. It took a long time, but I've done it."

"Your door is open?" He sounded incredulous.

"More or less. I'll be able to get out without any trouble when it's safe. Look, I'll prove it to you. I'll come to your spy-hole tomorrow evening."

"What have you done all this for?"

"For the reasons I told you the other day. I don't want to go out of my mind. I don't want to accept my imprisonment like so many of them do, to become a mere vegetable. I want to give myself at least the feeling of freedom. And perhaps—"

He interrupted. "How did you manage to dismantle a great thick heavy door like that?"

"It took some doing," I admitted.

"You might be caught."

"If the door was slammed really hard, perhaps. But I'm on the look-out. With any luck I'll always be able to shut it myself."

"Look out," he whispered. "I can hear a noise in the corridor. Get down quick."

We scrambled back to our cells.

The next morning, when we went out to exercise, Jeantet threw a quick and furtive glance at my door. He spotted the hanging towel, and looked at me. When we came back he examined his own door for some time; but he obviously had not solved the mystery.

I thought: He doesn't know whether to believe me or not. Despite that, I was sure he had passed his crisis.

It never occurred to me for a moment what gross imprudence it would be to go out; and if it had, I should not have cared. I waited impatiently for nightfall. Restless, heart beating fast, I sat there till Montluc was folded in silence. Guards had been mounted in the courtyard; the lights outside were lit, and those in the building turned off. Soon I heard nothing but the usual prison night-sounds: an earth-commode being opened, the scrape of a bucket, someone coughing.

The factory clock outside the prison struck ten. I spread out a blanket on the concrete, in front of the door; and gently, taking great care, began to dismantle the central panel. I knocked out the wedges which held the "shutter," removed the "shutter" itself, and then, gripping the loose board at its top end, pulled it into the cell. The wood creaked slightly, and then gave without any trouble. Some fragments of the tenons I had cut through fell out on to the blanket, so I cleared the mortises on both sides completely.

Next, using my spoon-handle, I slid the nearest board on the right into the vacant space and pulled that out too. As before, I cleared the severed strips of deal away from the mortises, both in the board itself and the door-frame. Then the whole operation was repeated on the left-hand board. This done, I was confronted with a gaping hole, a kind of wicket-gate, through which I could clearly see the gallery railing. Beside me, within easy reach, all the pieces of wood were neatly laid out, in the order in which I had removed them.

I took a deep breath and put my head through the aperture, like a rat at the mouth of its hole. For a moment I crouched there on all fours, listening. It was an extraordinary feeling, this solitary communion with limitless space. The whole place seemed to belong to me, and drew me on irresistibly.

I turned on my side and slowly wriggled out into the corridor— first an arm, then my body, then the other arm, and so on. Finally I found myself standing in the gallery. A solitary lamp on the ground floor shed its weak light upward from floor to floor. It was a clear night outside, but the moon hardly penetrated the long central skylight above my head. I stood motionless in the shadows, alert for danger, ready to dart back into my cell at the least noise.

I stared, absorbed, round the empty building; the experience afforded me a sensation of quite indescribable pleasure. It was, I suppose, somewhat akin to what a mountaineer feels when he at last reaches the summit after a hard and dangerous climb. Then

I slowly stole down the passage to Jeantet's cell, and put my face close to the spy-hole.

"Eugene! Eugene!" I whispered through the aperture. My voice seemed horribly loud in the silence.

Eugene turned over on his mattress, but made no reply. Baffled in my attempts to share my pleasure, and not daring to call him again, I went back to my cell and at once began to put the door together again.

At first light, when the guards began to blow their whistles, I got up to make sure that I had done the job properly. All the debris I had stripped from the boards and frame during the night went into the bucket.

When we went out for exercise I asked Eugene if he had heard anything during the night. He shook his head.

"I came to your spy-hole," I said.

"Why?"

"To show you I could get out if I wanted to."

He said: "Come up to the fanlight this evening."

In the wash-house I broke my good news to Nathan, who warned me to be careful. I could only exchange a word or two with him: the prisoner who occupied the cell opposite mine had joined the queue immediately behind me, and was now at the next tap. He looked at me, then suddenly said, in a low voice which no one could overhear: "Do you want to escape?"

"Me? How could I do that?" My answer came a little too quickly.

"Then what about your door? What were you doing in the gallery last night?"

"Getting some fresh air."

"Don't worry—and keep your temper. The one thing I want to do is to escape. Listen. I've got a plan—"

"Careful: the guard's watching us."

A little while later he went on: "Meet me in here each morning. I'll tell you how I mean to do it. We could make a break together."

It was from that moment on that I began to look carefully at the walls and the roof.

The prison acquired new inmates every day; the gaps left by those moved to Fresnes or Compiègne were soon filled. Few cells remained empty. Soon the Germans organised morning exercise by floors; this cut me off from Nathan, who lived below me. Some time before he had contrived to slip me a thousand-franc note. As he gave it to me he said: "I've got some money hidden away. Keep this. It may come in useful. One way or another you're going to escape: I'm convinced you'll get away somehow."

Martin, the black marketeer with tortoise-shell glasses and shifty eyes, had been drafted elsewhere. As he was voicing one last complaint before his departure I said to him, while we walked round the courtyard: "Things aren't so bad for you in here. They only send us out to be shot."

I could not help smiling at his miserable expression when he heard this.

Since I could no longer maintain contact with Nathan, I found myself seeing more and more of Roland de Pury. There were several reasons for this. To begin with he was a minister, a man of the Church. When death is in the air, the sinner tends to think of his soul's salvation, and take some comfort from guarantees of eternal life. Though the Abbé Bouvier, my parish priest, had found me a model pupil, I had abandoned all religious observances after growing up, and drifted into a somewhat indifferent attitude to Christianity. This problem worried me; I was relying on the minister to give me guidance.

Secondly, he was a Swiss. I did not believe his country would leave him to rot away in a French prison; it seemed probable that, sooner or later, he would be repatriated. This made him a potential messenger. Being the man he was, he would consider it his bounden duty to undertake any mission in his power which might be entrusted to him. We had, moreover, discovered common relations in Geneva. I was, finally, drawn to him by a certain quality of mysticism I sensed in his character, a generosity and sympathy inherent in his whole personality. As the days passed this attraction deepened into true friendship.

When he asked me what punishment I anticipated receiving, he realised at once that I had little hope of mercy.

"It is a serious matter, then?" he asked me.

"To you, as a minister, it must seem serious, yes. I was arrested as a spy, and I am charged with attempting to destroy certain important installations which the Germans are using."

"Have they proof of this?"

"All the proof in the world. A German agent got into our organisation and revealed the whole affair."

"Have you a family?"

"Three children—two in North Africa, one still in Savoy. Have you?"

"I have five children here in Lyons."

This was our first real contact, and for the time we left it at that. But it paved the way for more intimate confidences. Soon de Pury knew everything there was to be known about my life and activities. He had, in return, told me the reasons which had led to his imprisonment. Like all of us, at first he found the enforced inactivity unbearable.

"If only I had a pencil!" he sighed.

I felt immediately in the lining of my trousers and gave him the one I had on me.

Gratitude and pleasure flooded into his face. This tiny object was going to play the same role in his life as a prisoner as the spoon-handle had done in mine; it was going to help his struggle against boredom and loneliness. My existence now changed its nature. Jeantet and de Pury had entered my life, and if the minister offered me a moral support, I did the same for Jeantet. I passed on to one what I received from the other. Perhaps I too would have slipped into their state of mental tranquillity, fortified by Divine Grace or sheer oblivion, if my secret door and the plans of my friend opposite had not occupied my mind night and day.

I have never known how or why it was that Brunoy, a former police inspector of Lyons, should have been put in that particular cell. He had heard me working on my door, had kept watch, and seen that though double-locked, it could nevertheless be "opened."

"I have a plan," he had told me.

The word "plan" affected me like an electric shock. Was escape possible after all, despite these high, well-guarded walls? Brunoy must be mad or dreaming. If a plan could be devised and put into action, surely I would have guessed it? Over days and weeks I had, as I thought, exhausted all the possibilities. There was, it seemed, someone in Montluc who was cleverer at this sort of thing than I was. Almost by instinct I found myself beside him in the wash-house next morning; I had fallen in behind him for morning exercise.

"You say you've got a plan—to escape from inside?" I asked the question in a stupefied voice.

"Yes, I have a plan. And I intend, as you say, to escape from inside the prison."

"Have you taken a good look at the walls and the sentries?"

"It is precisely because I have studied them very carefully that I have been able to devise my plan."

"If you're serious, you must be a genius."

He said: "Not quite. I'm like you. I want to get out."

Brunoy was clearly neither mad nor dreaming. Faced with his assurance I began to lose my scepticism.

"Come to the latrines at the same time as me tomorrow, and I'll explain it all to you," he said.

That evening, before I went to sleep, I crouched up at the fanlight, watching the dark silhouettes of the walls and the armed guards gradually fading into the darkness, wondering what Brunoy's plan could be.

5

In the end, what with departures and the reorganised system of morning exercise, I was restricted in my choice of friends to my own floor. Bury had gone now, and Nathan was inaccessible. But the minister, de Pury, was fortunately in a cell close to mine, number 119; and my immediate neighbour, Jeantet, occupied a good deal of my time. As for Brunoy, his irruption into my daily routine altered the course of his own existence no less than mine.

Tomorrow, he had said, you will know my plan.

At the beginning of our trek round the courtyard I took up a position immediately behind him, and managed later to join him in the latrines.

"Well?" I said to him, eagerly.

He said: "Have you noticed the procedure when we come into this courtyard? The two German guards let the column pass through ahead of them. About two or three minutes elapse before they rejoin us and take up their positions."

"Yes," I said thoughtfully, "you're right."

"We've got to take advantage of those two minutes when the courtyard's empty to slip away and hide."

"Where could we hide?"

"On the roof of the wash-house. It wouldn't be too difficult to climb up, it's not very high. Once we're up there, we've got plenty of cover. The next thing we have to do is work our way along the tiles till we get to the angle of the wall."

"How do we get over the two outer walls?"

"If you look carefully, you'll see a pretty solid-looking gutter running along the top. With a pair of ropes and grappling-irons there'd be no trouble at all."

"How on earth can we get ropes and grappling-irons?" I asked him.

"That's the problem. We need one to get into the sentries' perimeter, long enough to avoid the risk of crippling ourselves when we drop, and the other to scale the outer wall."

I said: "What we've got to do, then, is to find our climbing-aids, and keep fit enough to swarm up a twenty-five-foot rope."

"See what ideas you can think up. I've got half a notion already. Meet me here again tomorrow or the day after. We've got to work fast. I can't stand this hellish place much longer."

"I'm just as anxious to get out as you are," I said. "But this time we've got to succeed. And that means taking every possible precaution. We mustn't rush our preparations."

The roof of the wash-house was in a corner of the courtyard which I could observe from my fanlight. I could, therefore, apply my mind to Brunoy's scheme that evening. The route we would have to take stood out clearly—the place where we could hide, the line of the walls, the all-important guttering. But there was one nasty snag. The angle formed by the roof itself and the inner wall would, as Brunoy had said, camouflage our progress along the tiles, and our preparations for dropping over into the perimeter— *but only at ground level*. From his office or bedroom on the first floor, the Head Warder could only too easily look out and see the whole thing. This was all the more liable to happen since our attempt would be made during morning exercise—that is, at a time when he would be most likely to keep an eye on the court-yard.

And where were we to get our material for ropes and grappling-iron from? Ropes could be manufactured from blankets and bolster-covers; there was no insuperable problem there. But to find metal sufficiently strong for our purpose, and to make it into hooks—that was another matter altogether. And how could these hooks (supposing they could be made) be fastened to the ropes? There was a guard patrolling the perimeter; we should have to get down one wall and up the other in the time it took him to do three-quarters of his round. This plan, in fact, lacked two essential ingredients: enough time to put it into action, and darkness to conceal it.

I called Jeantet up to the fanlight, told him what we planned, and asked his advice.

"I want to try and escape again," I said. "At the same time I've got to plan the whole thing down to the last detail. Then, if I fail, I can't blame myself. Brunoy's plan deserves consideration. But I'm not particularly enthusiastic about capering along the tiles in broad daylight, and right under Fränzel's window."

"I don't quite understand."

I explained each step of the operation in detail, commenting on the difficulties as I went.

Eugene promised to think about the problem, and give me his considered opinion later. We retired for the night.

Next day I told Brunoy what I thought were the flaws in his plan.

I said: "Try and dismantle your door, too. Then we could escape by another route—and at night, which is the most important thing."

"Have you any suggestions?"

"Not yet. But there must be some way. It's too risky in broad daylight. Besides, your method calls for great speed. With two of us, the chances of escape would be halved."

Brunoy said: "I shall have a shot at it alone."

He saw that I was not over-enthusiastic, and that I would not join in such an escapade without most careful preliminary preparations. In our position patience seemed to me the prime virtue, and nervous haste a positive danger. Brunoy was to learn this the hard way.

He said nothing to me for several days afterwards, except that he found it impossible to dismantle his door; but I sensed that he was making his own preparations, and that they would have dramatic consequences.

One morning, as soon as the duty N.C.O. opened his door, I saw him move quickly down the gallery to get himself a place at the front of the column before we marched out. He's going to do it today, I thought, and felt my hands tremble with nervous anticipation. My throat was dry.

I dragged along slowly in the small courtyard to delay the guards and give Brunoy a few more seconds' respite; as soon as I came through into the main compound I saw that he had vanished. The parade that morning passed in an atmosphere of unusual quietness. Jeantet, who had noticed nothing, was busy calculating the height of the walls for my benefit.

When we came back inside the duty N.C.O. passed by the cell opposite mine without paying any attention to Brunoy's absence. There was nothing odd about this; every day some cell-doors were left open while the occupants were away being interrogated. As the minutes passed I felt my anxiety gradually changing to joy. This joy was shared by the whole floor, because the other prisoners had begun to pass the news on from one cell to the next.

I was just about to climb up to my fanlight when I was brought up short by a loud commotion down the corridor. Heavy footsteps and shouting voices grew louder as they approached my cell. I remembered what had happened on April 23, and was filled with almost unbearable pity.

Fränzel was cursing away, but seemed unusually out of breath. Two soldiers had Brunoy firmly by the arms, and now led him into his cell. I watched the scene through my spy-hole.

The poor devil took a terrible beating. I heard the thuds as he was kicked and blackjacked, even though the noise was half-deadened by the thick concrete walls. Brunoy groaned, and from time to time screamed horribly. I caught a glimpse of Fränzel; he was looking round the cell at the same time as he tortured Brunoy, and I realised he was punishing him partly for the destruction of cell-equipment which Brunoy had utilised in his attempt.

Still swearing, he slammed the door and locked it. He was in a furious temper. All he needs now, I thought, is to stumble on my false door. I could not help smiling at the thought; but cold sweat was trickling down my face.

"Will they shoot me?" Brunoy asked when Fränzel had gone.

"Surely not." But my reassurance was uneasy.

"My rope broke when I was half-way up. The guard caught me without firing a shot."

Someone was coming down the corridor. The duty sergeant. He opened Brunoy's cell, and I saw Brunoy standing there, motionless, his eyes fixed on the N.C.O.

A thin line of blood was trickling down one cheek.

He was taken away then, and his footsteps faded along the gallery, down the stairs. I sat on my bed, miserable, and began to think.

But after dinner, to my amazement, he was brought back.

"Well?" I said quickly, as soon as the German guard was out of sight.

"I have been interrogated."

"Where?"

"Gestapo headquarters."

"What did they say?"

"They're going to release me."

"I see," I said. A terrible suspicion formed in my mind. I said, urgency in my voice: "How did you make the grappling-irons?"

"With the metal from the lamp-shutter."

"And the ropes?"

"Strips of blanket tied end to end."

"Tell me what happened."

He said: "The grappling-hook caught first time, but the rope broke when I began to climb, and too high up to get it back."

"What appalling luck!"

"No, they're going to let me go. I was sent here by mistake."

We had to raise our voices somewhat to carry on a conversation from one door to the other. I knew everyone was listening, and began to be afraid that Brunoy would make some mention of my door. Accordingly I cut him short, and returned to my bed.

Shortly before supper, Fränzel came for him again. He went off quite cheerfully; he seemed to believe in the promise the Gestapo had made him.

I had about half-emptied my mess-tin of soup when a number of shots brought me up short, spoon poised in one hand. I sat in thought for a moment; looked at the door, then at my mess-tin; and went on with my wretched meal.

Everything was quite quiet now.

A little later, Jeantet rapped on the wall, and I went up to the skylight.

"That was Brunoy," he said.

"The shots came from the direction of the perimeter. They must have put him against the wall, and . . ."

Jeantet said: "It's horrible. But why did they tell him he would be released? He was so confident—"

"You don't know the Gestapo. No one can afford to be confident over anything in here. Poor devil, he never knew. He was happy right up to the last moment."

"That," said Jeantet grimly, "is the price of failure if you try to escape."

"Nonsense, Eugene. This is one extra reason for risking it. Brunoy was too impatient. His preparations were faulty. But his information was invaluable."

"Yes, I heard. The rope and the grappling-irons."

"His rope wasn't strong enough, and he let himself down into the perimeter. That was hopeless. From the angle of the wall where he was he could have thrown his rope right across to the outer wall. Then all he had to do was hook it on at the near end as well, and he could get out without touching ground in the perimeter at all."

"How?"

"Like a monkey—upside-down, head first, hanging on with his hands and feet."

Jeantet said: "So he could have made it. What a tragedy."

"Yes. But it's better to die that way if you've got to, looking them in the face. Brunoy is one more example for us to follow. Eugene, you've got to go on. A whole regiment doesn't stop when one man falls."

"Your cell door can be opened, you've found a way to get across the perimeter—but that isn't all—"

"How right you are, Eugene. There's a great deal more to think about yet."

Jeantet was showing himself more friendly and intimate; this delighted me. He was gradually becoming involved. The empty rooms in his heart were being furnished with sympathy, affection, and—for the enemy—hatred.

Brunoy's successor in the cell opposite was a very young man. He was seventeen, but looked at least two years less. The Gestapo was now imprisoning old men, women, and—though we did not know it yet—children. His name was Duflot.

"Poor kid!" murmured Jeantet, when Duflot appeared at his door before morning exercise.

Duflot stared at us, smiling. He had an unusually spirited air about him.

During our march round the courtyard I asked him what had brought him to Montluc.

He said: "Ask the Boches if you're so interested."

"I was simply surprised to see a boy of your age in prison."

He tapped his breast. "Do you suppose we've got nothing in there at seventeen?"

"Good. You're a fine lad. If I get out of here I'll take you with me as a soldier."

Afterwards I found out that he had been arrested for distributing leaflets, which he dropped even in hotels occupied by the Germans. His youth and poise, his indifference to the guards and N.C.O.s, the coarse jokes he made at their expense, all this made him a most sympathetic and attractive personality.

"Give me a cigarette," he said to the sergeant one day, stretching out his hand.

The latter, taken by surprise, pulled a packet out and gave him one.

"What about a match?"

The sergeant lit Duflot's cigarette, and then turned the key in his cell-door. He took two steps down the corridor, stopped short, scratched his head. Then he went on with his rounds.

Another prisoner was brought in about the same time, and put into cell 110 next door. From my spy-hole I could see both cells, and, to the right of them, the latrines serving this part of the second floor. They were no longer used for their original purpose; but, as I had found in my previous quarters, they contained some useful hiding-places.

The words chalked on the door behind which Duflot's new neighbour was installed immediately attracted my attention.

Kein essen, kein Ausgang, and then a date. No food; not to be let out.

All the privations I had endured in the condemned block were revived by this notice; hunger, thirst, the obsession with food, the wonderful dreams that make waking reality yet more terrible by contrast—all these I could feel behind that locked door only a few feet away.

And my own cell door was open!

When I heard ten o'clock chime out from the factory clock, I dismantled my door as I had done before, and went out into the gallery. This time I took the precaution of hanging my second blanket over the door, in case the moonlight, streaming in through the window, shone through that gaping hole on to the floor outside.

Then, after listening carefully, I went to the cell opposite and looked at the chalk inscription on the door. It stood out white against the stained oak. Very carefully I rubbed it out. I was taking a most imprudent step, and knew it; but I was obeying an uncontrollable impulse which was stronger than the dictates of reason.

The following morning the orderly sergeant opened this cell as as well as the others. When the occupant appeared at his door in handcuffs, I was terrified. But the sergeant merely glanced at the door itself, and then released the manacled hands stretched out towards him.

I gave a huge sigh of relief, and looked at our new companion with some enjoyment. Completely taken aback, he had joined our column. A new factor was now beginning to enter my considerations: the stupidity of our gaolers. I had only begun to explore its depths and usefulness.

The following night I went to his spy-hole once more, and called to him as quietly as possible.

"*Psst*, come here. Come to the spy-hole."

I heard him move, and repeated my request. He got up.

"Feeling better now?" I chuckled.

"Who are you?" He seemed completely panic-stricken, and his voice was far too loud.

"Don't worry. I'm one of your neighbours."

Confused, he said: "Come back again—please come back—but how can you get out—?"

I cut in quickly. "I'll come back—but only on condition that you talk more quietly."

Then I went back to my hole, and shut it.

When we came out of our cells the following morning, he studied every face in turn. When he saw the grin I could not prevent breaking out on my face, and the wet towel hung from my door, he knew I must be the night-walker who had disturbed his sleep. After that he could hardly take his eyes off me.

He seemed a resolute, pleasant, tough sort of fellow; even a possible companion for an escape.

I had no difficulty in talking to him; on his own initiative he got the next seat to me in the latrines. He told me his name was Mercier, and apologised for his confused state the previous night. I asked him why he was in Montluc.

"For the same reason as you, I should think."

"You were given away?"

"After a while, yes. By my wife."

He saw my surprise.

"Listen," he said, "it's a nasty story. I'll tell you about it, bit by bit. You'll see you can rely on me. But promise me one thing—take me with you. I know you're planning to escape. You've found some way of opening your door. You prowl about the building at night. Well, I want to escape as well, whatever the risk."

"There's no need to tell me your story if you don't want to. I trust you. The words chalked on your cell door told me all I needed to know."

"No," he said, "I must tell you. You'll understand me better then."

"Very well. I'll come to your spy-hole tonight. I'll give you a pencil and some paper. It'll be easier that way. You can write down anything you like. I'd like the pencil back."

Two days later, in the wash-house, he said to me: "Take my towel. Don't unfold it."

When I got back to my cell I found in the towel a small sheet of my paper. On it this was written:

I escaped from Germany. I risked my life countless times in order to get back home. I had hardly been married two months before I was sent to the front. When at last I made it, I found my wife living with another man. I went to his house. I wanted to kill her, but I couldn't. He began to apologise and make excuses for himself. I used every argument I could to try and make her come home. She refused. To stop me pestering her she denounced me. She can do a great deal of harm. She knows a good deal through me —I was a fool to trust her—and the Gestapo will get it out of her somehow. I have to do everything I can to protect my friends. For God's sake get me out of here.

"So you want to risk getting yourself killed?" I said to him next day as we washed.

"No more than you."

"There is little chance of success."

"One chance in a thousand is enough. I must try. I would be the most miserable creature on earth if I didn't have a shot at the impossible."

"Supposing we fail?"

"Don't worry," he said, "I won't disgrace you in front of the firing-squad."

I made my decision. "Meet me here again," I said. "I'll tell you the secret way I've found of getting through my door."

The look which we exchanged was worth all the affidavits and oaths in the world.

There still remained the problem of how to get out of the central block itself. All the doors were locked during the night; the sergeant-major and the duty sergeant slept on the first floor, the corporal below them. Inside the building there were no patrols or sentries; only one weak lamp broke the gloom, and even this was not always lit. It would be difficult enough to open a locked door without a key. But beyond this door there was a guarded courtyard, surrounded by high walls with a patrolled perimeter on the far side. It seemed an impossible situation, enough to damp anyone's enthusiasm.

I examined every plan in turn, straightforward and dangerously complicated alike. Over one of them I lingered for a considerable time. Its basic aim was to attack and neutralise the guard-house, and it consisted of three distinct stages. First, I had to get control of the central block; next, to eliminate the sentries in the courtyard; lastly, attack the guard-room itself.

The first part of this operation would be the most difficult. I would leave my cell, go down to the first floor, and cut the throats of Fränzel and the sergeant while they were asleep. (I would have to obtain Grimaud's razor somehow.) I would take a gun from one of them. Then I would go down to the ground floor and deal with the corporal in the same way. I should have to rely on none of them being awake. Next, I would go back to the first floor and release de Pury. We would open the doors into the courtyard, and de Pury, who spoke German fluently, would call the guards into the building one after the other. Meanwhile we would have set Nathan and Mercier free; they would knock out the sentries, strip them of their arms, and lock them in a cell under strict supervision to ensure that they made no noise.

After this I would open some more cells, arm a few carefully chosen prisoners, and lead an attack on the unsuspecting police post. We could then deal with the sentries in the perimeter. The scheme needed some preliminary reconnaissance; in particular I would have to find out whether Fränzel, the sergeant and the corporal locked their doors at night.

I realised that to succeed, this operation would require such a combination of discipline and luck that it could only be considered as a last, desperate resort. Either it would come off completely, in which case every prisoner in Montluc would be free; or it would fail absolutely, and I should not only be shot myself, but involve a large number of my fellows in a similar fate.

In the light of later events, and considering such escapes as were, in fact, made from Montluc, I believe this bold scheme might have had some success. Certainly if every prisoner had been able, at that time, to foresee his future, more than one door would have been broken down, and there would have been no lack of volunteers to join me.

I also toyed with the idea of stealing noiselessly into the corporal's room and getting hold of his keys. This would have enabled me to open one of the gates in the courtyard; but the notion came to nothing in the end, and I abandoned it. I looked for sewers, but failed to find any; I do not believe there were any in Montluc, for we emptied our buckets down an ordinary drain in the middle of the courtyard.

There still remained the roof.

Our latest recruit was a railwayman. I must have appeared friendly, because the first morning he joined in the trek round the courtyard he tried to ask me the usual ritual questions: what was my name, where was I from, what was going to happen to me. He was not a Savoyard by birth, but had more or less become one by adoption; his wife came from Saint-Jeoire-en-Faucigny, and every year he spent his holidays in this pleasant and picturesque resort.

He was a likeable man. He was always cursing the Germans, quietly but with immense fervour; his hatred was sharpened by the necessity for concealing it. He was an old man, white-haired. He told me that the Gestapo had got nothing out of him, and he would probably be released. This was what, in fact, later happened.

I had taken the opportunity, at his suggestion, of giving him a message for my family. He hid it inside one sock. This message reached my family a few days later and puzzled them considerably. In it I asked them for some linen shirts, and told them to be sure and do up the parcels with long, thick string.

While I was working out the various problems I had to solve, I was also making experiments in manufacturing rope. I decided to use my bolster-cover. I teased out what little horse-hair stuffing it contained, and hid it in my mattress. Then I set about the cover itself. I cut it into broad strips, and folded these in four thicknesses, turning the edges in so that they would not fray. These folded strips I twisted into a rope, and bound with wire from my bedstead, taking care to twist the wire in the opposite direction. This preserved the torsion. The experiment seemed quite satisfactory.

That evening I shut the skylight, and tied my piece of rope to a window-bar. Then I hung on it with my full weight, and gave it several violent tugs. Despite its slenderness, it resisted all my attempts to snap it. This encouraged me to go on with what, I knew, would be a long and niggling job. The bolster-cover was made of pure linen, and reminded me of the huge pile of shirts—also of linen—which had belonged to my grandfather, and probably to his father before him. They had always been kept in a special wardrobe in our family house.

String, I judged, would be better for my purposes than wire; that was why, in the letter Schoeller had passed on, I asked for these family shirts in carefully-tied parcels. For the same reason, I gave no explanation of my curious requirements.

As the days passed, my plan of escape took root and grew in me; it became a part of my life. My mind dwelt on it more and more continuously, to the point of obsession. The initial impossibilities it presented were being overcome. Little by little the belief that I would really get away with it crystallised in my mind, thanks to my increased knowledge of the prison's topography, the experiments I had already made, the theories I had evolved, and my own growing self-confidence. Every night, alone in the gallery, the silent reaches of the prison around me, I breathed in the air of freedom; each fresh move was a step nearer the end of the tunnel. Elated, I felt the compelling need to go yet further. When I returned to my cell and reassembled my door, I was conscious of new strength coursing through my entire body.

I had quite a lot on my side: an increasingly determined urge to escape, a plan already sketched out in broad outline and partially realised, the stupidity of the Germans, and a certain congenital predisposition to good luck on which I had always consciously drawn. There were two elements in this plan: mine and God's. Where, I wondered, was the dividing-line set?

Alas, I could not tell; but I felt that heaven would only aid my grimly resolute struggle insofar as I threw every physical and moral reserve I possessed into the balance.

The sign from heaven came about the end of June, in a completely unexpected way. The weather grew more and more sultry; in our concrete cage the heat increased the natural stink which always hung about the cells. Fränzel found himself bothered by this warm, fetid atmosphere, and had the big skylight in the roof opened. Through my spy-hole I saw a soldier with a long crank working the system of rods which controlled this skylight. Slowly it jerked open, revealing the blue sky beyond it.

That evening I said to Eugene: "I'm going out on the roof to-night."

"How?"

"You must have heard the noise in the gallery this morning. They've opened the big skylight. I'm going to climb through it."

"Why do you want to go out on the roof? You might be caught."

"To see if my plan is possible."

"Have you got a ladder?"

"Don't be funny. You know the iron bar that runs up the wall, the one that opens and shuts the skylight? I'm going to climb up that."

"It's very high."

"Listen, Eugene: I've got to know if I can get out this way. If I can, it's another step forward."

"Another step to freedom—or death."

I said: "Living can be a risky business, Eugene."

The skylight was long and narrow, and indistinguishable in shape and colour from the other double windows in the roof. It was controlled by this system of rods I have mentioned, which were worked by a ratchet mechanism. The first rod emerged from a square box in which the crank was inserted, and ran vertically up the wall between two cell doors. The second ran at right angles from it across the ceiling. Its further end engaged with a serrated bar, slightly curved, which supported the window-frame, raising or lowering it like a trap-door. The skylight itself was encased in a strong metal frame. The rods were held in place by ring-joints cemented into the wall. These rings gave the ratchet free play and allowed the rods to revolve.

The open skylight was about twelve feet above the top floor, directly over the gallery. If the rod or anything else gave while I was climbing, I ran the risk of falling over the banisters to the ground below. I had not failed to notice, too, how thin these iron rods were. Even if I succeeded in getting to the edge of the skylight, I knew it would require a remarkable athletic feat to pull myself through it on to the roof. The ratchet-bar was going to get in my way, and I should have to go round it one side or the other. I would have to take care as I did so that my weight rested on the metal framework, not on the glass itself.

This was a challenge worth taking up. Looking through the spy-hole I weighed up my chances. I knew that once night fell, the demonic impulse that drove me on would let no argument, however logical, stand in its way. Somehow or other the thing would be done.

I planned to go out of my cell at ten o'clock. If, an hour later, I was neither on the roof nor lying below with all my bones broken, it would be due to cowardice and nothing else.

Pride and obstinacy lent me all the courage I needed. I was determined to go on; I was determined to conquer what appeared an insurmountable difficulty, both to take my plan one step further and win a moral victory.

When ten o'clock struck, I was standing under the skylight.

As on previous nights, nothing disturbed the silence inside the building. The metal rod stood out clearly against the whitewashed wall. In the dim light that filtered up to the gallery from the central well I could make out the bolt and lock of the door on the left, and the hinges of the next one, to the right of the rod. Above my head I could see the sky through the open aperture; it drew me irresistibly. I was once more alone in these familiar surroundings, master of my actions and my immediate future.

I grasped the rod with both hands. It creaked dismally in its rings; luckily the noise could easily be mistaken for a bucket scraping on the floor. I pulled myself up like a gymnast on a bar, and then, shifting my hands, repeated the performance; this got me high enough to find a foothold on the metal ledges that projected above the doors on either side. After that I went on up like a caterpillar, pushing with my feet and pulling with my arms, till I reached the top of the vertical rod.

The second horizontal rod looked horribly thin and fragile. I breathed in deeply, aware of the sheer drop that yawned below me.

Now for the worst part. With one hand I grasped the rim of the frame that surrounded the skylight. Then I slowly worked my legs up till they were resting on the horizontal rod, and occupying the narrow space that separated it from the ceiling. This done, I could move my other hand to a position close beside the first. I was now hanging horizontally above a sheer drop, my back to the ground and the rod pressed into my chest. Gritting my teeth, scarcely daring to breathe, I edged back inch by inch towards the open skylight, gripping the ledge firmly with both hands, till my body was bent like a jack-knife. I got my head through, and then the upper part of my body. Shifting my grip a little, I lowered my legs from the rod and let them dangle in mid-air.

There above me was the huge, starry night; red lights twinkled away into the distance along the railway line.

Limitless space.

Mouth wide open, I gaped at this wonderful sight. I decided to get into a slightly more comfortable position; to do this I shifted one hand to the edge of the skylight itself, with the idea of pulling myself up a little further. A small piece of glass broke under the pressure of my fingers and jingled down noisily on to the roof.

Motionless and terrified, I hung there listening. What would happen? A few inaudible words floated up to me from the courtyard; then all was still once more.

For what seemed an eternity I remained in this position, not daring to move a finger, soaked with sweat, my heart beating violently. I was paralysed with fright. A train eventually came to my rescue. It gave a long blast on its whistle as it approached, noisily shattering the silence of the night. I took advantage of this lucky chance to slide back through the aperture and down the iron rods. They creaked horribly under my weight. The train was still steaming slowly into the near-by station when eleven o'clock struck.

Back in my cell I realised how much malnutrition and lack of exercise had sapped my strength. I quickly fell asleep, with every star that shines in the firmament bright in my mind's eye, and the pure evening air still filling my lungs.

The following morning I saw traces of my ascent on the wall; the whitewash had been marked by my feet and knees. But who would guess how those marks had got there, or even notice them? In fact, only Duflot did; he asked me about them later.

I now knew it was possible to get on to the roof by way of the skylight. But how could I proceed from the roof to the walls without being seen? The block was three storys high. The cells measured between ten and eleven feet from floor to ceiling; that added up to about thirty-five feet. Allowing for the thickness of the floors, and other extras, I assumed—to be on the safe side—that the roof was well over forty feet from the ground.

That evening Jeantet knocked on my wall. I went up to my fan-light.

"What was going on last night?" he asked. "You made a lot of noise."

"I climbed up to the roof, through the skylight."

"How does that help you?"

"At the moment, not very much. I've still got to find some way of getting down into the courtyard without being seen."

"It needs thought."

I agreed.

During the next few days he examined the walls carefully, esti-mated the height of the roof, counted the number of drain-pipes which ran down from it, and noted their positions.

Everything in his attitude showed both keen interest in the prob-lem and an obvious desire to appear optimistic.

"We'll solve it, don't you worry," he would say. "We'll join your two ends up for you. Now look at that gutter . . ."

He was trying his hardest to be of use to me. No, he said, I couldn't rely on the drain-pipes. They lay too close to the walls, and were too exposed. Even supposing I could slide down one, it was very improbable that I could get a firm grip on it in the first place, since the edge of the roof protruded nearly three feet beyond the wall.

In the end it became clear that here, too, only a rope firmly at-tached to the roof would serve my purpose. That meant two new problems to discuss: first, the length of the rope and the material from which it should be made; next, how and where it should be used.

The cells, as I have said, were about eleven feet high. By adding to the sum of the three storys the thickness of the floors and the distance from the parapet to the point where I would fix the rope, and subtracting from this figure my own height, I reached a round total of thirty-three feet. This was alarming; it would require a very strong rope indeed to bear my weight over such a length. But since I could think of no better way, and Heaven on this occasion re-mained indifferent, I decided to adopt it.

As we went down the staircase to our morning exercise, we could see the flat roof of the guard-house through the window. This roof was made of concrete and covered with tarred shingle; it extended a short way beyond the wall to keep off heavy rain. It had a raised edge all round it, and was furnished with more solid and prominent guttering than the main walls. From the outside the roof of the central block closely resembled that of the guard-house both in shape and general dimensions. I inferred from this that they were actually constructed on the same lines. If this was so, it would be possible to hook a rope on to the parapet at any point—or, to be precise, on the narrow front that faced the military court-house.

I had observed from the courtyard that this frontage and the wall of the small building used as an infirmary were only a few feet apart; they formed a "blind angle" which would be invaluable to me for concealing my descent from the roof. Everything pointed to this side of the prison; not only the concealed face, but the wall of the infirmary yard, which would be easy to scale, and from which I could reach the roof of the covered gallery. This in its turn offered access to the outer wall itself, which gradually lost height as it passed the buildings used by the Courts Martial Tribunal.

I knew this part of the compound well; though I had never been over it in person I had spent much time examining it from the fan-light of my condemned cell. From my new quarters I could still carefully scrutinise the red-tiled roof, in fact the whole area; it was scarcely fifty yards away.

"Only fifty yards," I said to Eugene, "but it might as well be fifty miles. It'd be easier to cross Europe and Asia on foot than that courtyard."

"Perhaps. But in the latter case you wouldn't feel you'd won such a great victory."

His words moved me considerably.

I could do nothing till I had the necessary equipment. For the descent into the courtyard I needed a thirty-four-foot rope with a grappling-iron on the end; to cross the perimeter required another one nearly as long, and two more grappling-irons. To get them would need such calculations, research, experimenting and patience as it is hard to imagine. To begin with, the basic material available was scanty in the extreme. I had two blankets, my mattress-cover, a little personal linen, the wire from my bedstead, the metal frame enclosing the glass in front of my light, and two rudimentary tools —a sharpened spoon and a razor-blade. I should have to work very carefully, and be prepared to hide all my preparations at a second's notice.

Despite the odds against me, I set to work.

6

From the beginning of July our daily morning exercise was considerably shortened. We went out now in groups of ten, and soon the time spent on these sorties was a quarter of an hour or less. My group comprised the prisoners at my end of the wing, among them such old hands as Jeantet, de Pury, Grimaud, Mercier and Duflot. Our supervision also became more strict. Fränzel had acquired the irritating habit of snooping along the galleries throughout the day in slippers. His idea was to peer in through the spy-holes and catch friends talking through the fanlights, or tapping out messages on their cell walls. Then he would fling the door open, knock the culprit about, and make him put his bed outside in the corridor.

I was lucky to occupy the far end of the wing, since there was always ample warning of Fränzel's approach. He never got this far without catching somebody; and after that his presence was no secret.

We were never searched. Our gaolers must have thought such a precaution superfluous. They censored all parcels that came in; the windows and doors were well-barred, the walls were high, the guards numerous and—so they thought—efficient.

Yet I took them in the whole time. I got my daily breath of fresh

90

air up at my fanlight; I went out into the gallery at night; I ex-changed information with my neighbours; I even cheated them over the soup-ration.

Meals were served out as follows. A fatigue-party brought up the soup to the landing in hay-boxes, which preserved some of its warmth. They also provided piles of mess-tins and a box of spoons. As the duty N.C.O. unlocked each door, the occupant came for-ward to take his ration. This was brought him by an orderly, several of whom shuttled to and fro between the cells and the hay-boxes. If one of them had given out the last mess-tin he carried, and the man who followed him did not notice, I would quickly put my ration down inside the door and stand hopefully waiting for more. I almost always got it.

In this way I obtained a double ration two or three times a week. This was very necessary for the success of my plans; I only realised after my climb up to the roof how much these weeks of confine-ment had weakened me. Afterwards I would calmly put both empty mess-tins out in the corridor; nobody ever asked me to ex-plain why there were two of them.

Mercier was still waiting for me to approach him again. He watched my least gesture and hung on my every word. Of all those there he certainly seemed the fittest to share the risks which my attempt would entail: his physical condition, his youth, the energy I sensed in him, not to mention the confidence he had shown in me, all marked him out as my potential companion. But with Brunoy's unfortunate fate in my mind, I still hesitated to admit him to the venture. He would have unreservedly given me all the help he could; he was ready for anything; but had I the right to accept that help when the chances of success were so slight?

He settled this matter of conscience for me himself, one morning in the wash-house.

"Take me with you!" he said, for the hundredth time; and there was such a pleading look in his face that, without any more hesita-tion, I explained the secret of the door to him.

"Take great care," I advised him. "Be very patient and very watchful."

He attacked his door with such zest that his neighbours and I spent all day begging him to stop.

He would pause for a few seconds, and then begin scraping, sawing and wrenching at the wood once more. Loud cracks echoed through the wing. Half-dead with fright, I tried to curb his enthusiasm.

"Careful, Mercier, you're making too much noise."

"Mercier, for God's sake stop it. You'll be caught."

"All right, that's enough for today."

But nothing would stop him. In one day, heaven knows how, he had managed to loosen one board completely. But that evening, while the soup was being distributed, the duty N.C.O. slammed his door particularly hard, and the board fell out.

Fränzel appeared a few moments later, Mercier was given a terrible thrashing and taken away.

I sat on my bed and ate my soup slowly, alert for the least sound, raising the spoon slowly to my lips, hardly breathing.

I had unwittingly done as much harm to Mercier as I had to Brunoy. Once again I was alone, faced with the entire responsibility for my plan.

For two or three days I remained reasonably calm. Then I went through a nasty nervous crisis, partly due to the dramatic loss of my friend, and partly to thinking about my family. It was a year since I had left my wife and children at Port Lyautey. The emotional confusion which seized me momentarily made me long to be with my family; I dreamed of my two boys, of our pleasant house in the Rue Petit-Jean, of the happy home-life I had once known.

Ever since I was a child I have loved animals and country life. In Port Lyautey every room in our flat looked out on an internal courtyard covered with ivy and broad-leafed garden vines where lizards hid. We had even made friends with a chameleon. Every evening we could see him on the wall in the lamp-light, hunting for flies. He would watch his victim for some time out of huge faceted eyes, and then seize him with a lightning dart of his long tongue. The pleasant July weather contributed to my melancholy mood, and made me look back with even greater longing to such pleasant moments.

How could I, a man of action born and bred, become sentimental over the memory of blonde hair, sweet-scented flowers, or the activities of lizards? I had to summon up all my pride and determination in order to counteract this at times all-enveloping emotion, and prevent myself lapsing into a state of chronic lassitude. Nor could I afford to forget how grim was the prospect before me.

7

The wire netting of my bedstead provided me with about fifty yards of tough, supple wire. I teased it out piece by piece, first of all removing the staples with which it was fastened to the wooden frame. Then I carefully straightened the wire I thus obtained, with my bare hands, and hid it under the covering of my mattress. I was careful to leave several threads in place so that the mattress stayed at its normal level.

My cell was never untidy. It was always well swept, and the few possessions I had were neatly lined up in one corner. Whenever I heard someone coming down the corridor, I would sit down on the bucket, or the edge of my bed, head in hands, and lose myself in a carefully-posed reverie. The wall where the light was extended beyond the field of observation offered by the spy-hole. It was in this corner that I went about my long, tiring task; and I could quickly push everything out of sight behind the bed.

All my shirts, drawers and handkerchiefs were sacrificed and turned into string. With the help of a razor-blade I cut them into narrow strips, which I then plaited tightly to increase their strength. As each length was completed I hid it in my bedding, which was rapidly turning into a kind of storehouse.

I spent many days on this preparatory task, and as yard followed yard my wretched stock of clothes literally vanished through my

94

fingers. The mattress-cover might just about give me enough material for the shorter, thirty-foot rope; but even the bolster-cover and my two blankets combined would not be sufficient to construct the longer one. And it was with this rope that I had to get down from the roof. To avoid wasting time I turned to another pressing problem: the fabrication of my grappling-irons.

At a suitable moment, when everything was quiet, I stood my bedstead up against the wall. It was now somewhat weakened by the removal of its wire; but I managed to climb up on to the top bar. This gave me access to the little window set across the niche in the wall which housed my light. I opened the window, took it off its hinges, and quickly scrambled down, hugging my precious burden to me.

Then I put bedstead and mattress back in their place, and examined the lamp-window closely.

The frame was two feet long, and a little more than a foot wide. It was made of thick iron strips, with a shallow channel cut along the inner edge. The ground glass panel fitted into this channel, and was held in place by a lead filling. The strips were joined at each corner by a small bracket containing two screws.

I knocked out the glass—I could not avoid making some noise during this operation—broke it into small pieces, and put these into my bucket. The following morning I emptied them down the drain past which we filed every day. (We walked as slowly as possible so as to make our time in the open air last a little longer.)

With my spoon-handle, which was proving itself a most adaptable tool, I gouged out the lead from the channels, and unscrewed the four brackets, carefully keeping the screws. This gave me four separate metal strips. Then I took my pencil and sketched a design for my three grappling-irons on the wall, taking care to make the mouth of each hook wide enough for my purposes. I possessed four iron strips with which to execute these designs. For many long days, taking extra care not to be spotted, I devoted myself to this tricky job.

I slid the end of the strip through the space between the closet-door and the huge bolt used to shut it. This gave me excellent leverage; exerting all the pressure of which I was capable, I managed to bend the strip into the right shape. But the metal was extremely resistant, and it took many attempts before I succeeded in converting the two longest strips into something resembling a grappling-iron. Time and again the strip would spring out of my hand with a frightful metallic clatter, and nearly make me jump out of my skin in fright. Whenever this happened I was sure someone would discover what I was doing. I would frantically hide all my apparatus, and sit listening while the minutes dragged by.

There remained the third grappling-iron. This was a more difficult proposition than the other two. It had to be made out of the two shorter strips, and these were particularly hard to bend because they offered less purchase. Nevertheless, I succeeded in this case as well; the third hook turned out no worse than the other two either in design or reliability. It was, indeed, considerably heavier; I had used nearly three yards of wire to lash the two component parts together.

The wire also enabled me to fashion three stout loops, one of which I attached to each hook. One of the grappling-irons still had its hinges attached to it, and it was easy enough to anchor the loop on to them. With the two others I experienced considerable difficulty, but managed to find a way in the end. When everything was finished, I hung the grappling-irons by their hooks on the ledge below the skylight and pulled as hard as I could. I even threaded the lines attached to the loops through the closet bolt, and used the latter as a kind of pulley in an effort to make them give. To my delight, I failed to make any impression on them.

When I had completed my test, I hid the grappling-irons on the outer ledge of my window. Jeantet, intrigued, tapped on the wall. We had a quick conversation through the fanlight.

"What are you doing?" he asked. "Where are you? You're so quiet I was getting worried."

"My grappling-irons are finished. They're very strong."

"They'll squeak on the concrete," he said. "You ought to sheath them in cloth to muffle the noise."

"That's a good idea. I won't forget it. But now I've got to think about ropes. I need about sixty-five feet of rope, Eugene."

"Sixty-five feet!"

"Thirty to cross the perimeter, thirty-five to get down off the roof."

"What are you going to make them out of?"

"My mattress-cover and blankets."

"You'll have to make the knots very strong," he began. Then, alarmed by some noise or other, he scuttled back into his cell.

The next day he waited till the guard had his back turned, and tossed a folded blanket into my cell. I quickly put it away and gave him a grateful smile. A day or two later he repeated the manœuvre. I began to wonder how many blankets he had.

As I passed in front of his cell-door on the way to exercise, I saw that his mattress was bare. That evening, up at the fanlight, I said to him: "You've given me both your blankets. You're going to be horribly cold at night. What's more, if I'm caught, and the Germans hold an enquiry, they'll find out that you helped me, and you'll be shot too. I won't have you taking such risks. I'll give you back your blankets tomorrow."

"No," he said sharply. "I've thought it all out. You haven't enough material to make your ropes. We all stick together here. We share a common struggle . . ."

I was very moved. "I remember, Eugene," I said; I vividly recalled having used these or similar words a few weeks before, to him. "But I don't need two blankets. One will be enough. I can give you back the other one without any trouble."

"I worked out that you needed—"

"I don't. Please believe me. I'll let you have it tomorrow morning."

He said: "I've made you a piece of rope myself, with my bolster-cover—"

"Eugene . . ."

I could not go on; I was choking with emotion.

When I set about making the thirty-five-foot rope, I found I had a formidable job on my hands. The mere length made it difficult enough; but I was also using my blankets now, and they proved awkward material to handle. I also reckoned to use the wire to preserve the torsion of each length, to strengthen the knots, and to reinforce weak sections; I found, however, that this made the rope rather stiff and, as a result, very difficult to conceal. I was keeping the string and the linen from the mattress for the other rope. If it was going to be thrown across the perimeter like a lasso, it would need to be light and flexible.

I cut each blanket into strips, lengthways. They were made of thick, loose-textured material which was not very strong. This meant that the strips had to be fairly wide. That was why I only made three strips out of each blanket. To begin with I tried a new system. I folded the edges of each strip into the middle till they were touching, and then folded them in two once more. This gave me four thicknesses of material, which I then twisted as hard as I could. Next I took the wire and bound it round in the opposite direction, which kept the torsion as firm as possible. This gave me a kind of long sausage which was strong enough, to be sure, but extremely bulky.

As a result the first join presented some tricky problems. An ordinary knot was out of the question; the loose ends kept slipping out of my hands. In the end I used a somewhat more simple method. I laid the two ends side by side, overlapping for quite a way, and then lashed them tightly together. This involved two interlocking loops. I anchored a double strand of wire to the first piece of rope, passed it through both loops, and then fastened it to the next section. This considerably strengthened the joint.

My mind was constantly obsessed by the fear of forgetting some essential factor. I hesitated before going on with any piece of work with which I was not completely satisfied, which meant that each section of the rope had to be tested individually. This could only be done at night, because it entailed exposing all my material. With this in mind I always left the fanlight wide open, as if I wanted to air my cell thoroughly. I had noticed as I went to and fro for exercise, that several other prisoners did the same thing. There was then, no extra risk involved in this. I tied the end of the rope round a window-bar and pulled at it with all my strength, shaking and jerking it. The rope occasionally stretched a little, but always held.

The next morning, as I worked it inch by inch into my mattress, I gave it a fresh inspection, and reinforced any weak points I noticed.

To lessen the number of knots and make the rope firmer, I alternated the sections made out of blanket with others in which I had employed towels. This material was lighter, and produced rope which was simultaneously thinner and tougher.

Jeantet was passionately interested in my activities, and kept himself informed of each fresh advance in the work. Every evening he called me up to the fanlight on the pretext of giving me some piece of advice; but I knew very well that this was not the real reason. He was living each scene of the drama himself, and my silence threw him into an agony of anxiety. Our conversations were now very short; I was becoming more and more afraid that Fränzel would catch us talking, throw out my bed into the corridor, and discover the absence of its wire-netting. This would have inevitably led to his also finding the rope, the grappling-irons, and my dismantled door.

I still went out every night, however. Alert for any sound, I would creep along to the main landing, absorbing the sensation of freedom which this open space and the absence of my guards gave me. Then, refreshed and fortified, I would return to my cell. Eugene took me to task for this habit. Duflot thought I was mad. They could not understand that I needed danger as other people need drugs; it acted as a stimulant, counteracting the enormous nervous exhaustion which the strain and anxiety of the last few months had produced in me.

So, despite all hazards, every day inserted a new stone into my edifice. Yet I knew it was built over a powder-mine that the smallest spark could set off.

8

The Annemasse tram was an hour late. The old
man was waiting in the Café Rigaud, near the
station. He sat there, his parcel beside him, a
brandy within easy reach, and rested himself after his long morning walk. As he passed through the villages on his way, he had
met one or two acquaintances. They, observing his distrait air
and the parcel he carried, realised that something serious was in
the air; though they could not, at the time, guess what.

But to M. Rigaut, one of his oldest friends, he told the truth. "I
found out last night that my son's been arrested. I'm going to see
what's happening."

"Which son?"

"André, the Army officer."

"Perhaps they picked him up simply because he'd been an
officer?"

"No," said the old man. "It was the German police who arrested him at Annemasse. We're occupied by the Italians. He
must have done something serious."

"Where is he?"

"In prison in Lyons."

"He'll probably get out somehow. He's been in some nasty
fixes already and come through all right."

"This time I'm really worried. He must have been behaving like a hooligan."

The tram pulled up outside, and hooted dismally. The old man got up and walked out to catch it.

He had not visited Lyons since he had been in hospital there, after being wounded during the first World War. But the names of Brotteaux and Perrache suddenly carried him back thirty years; he saw his younger self, in uniform, climbing these same steps, wandering along the same wharfs and streets as he had done so often in the distant past.

He stopped in front of the station, at the top of the steps, and recognised the main street and the square immediately in front of him. Among the hurrying travellers were several German soldiers, waiting for a train or about to return to barracks. He stared at them for a long time with intense curiosity. A taxi-cyclist offered to take him to his destination in the little trailer he towed behind his machine; the old man refused in disgust. He slowly walked down the steps, turned left till he reached the river, crossed by a foot-bridge, and began to climb the hill. Finally he reached a small square, found the school he was looking for, and rang the bell.

Jean Cambus was out, but was due back for an evening class about two hours later. The old man decided to wait. He sat down on a bench in the vestibule, directly under the bust of some haughty, moustachioed pedagogue who seemed to have stepped out of another world. The hall-porter, full of respect for this fine old countryman, and anxious to be of service to him, told him after a while that Professor Cambus had returned.

Cambus was a youngish man, very tall, brown and thin.

"My name is Devigny," the old man said. "Mme. Deletraz told me my son had been arrested, and I came to find out what was happening."

Cambus said: "We can't talk here. Come up to my room. I live on the premises. We'll be more comfortable there."

Their steps echoed down long bleak corridors, with class-rooms opening off them. Most of the class-rooms were empty. Cambus' room was obviously that of an intellectual bachelor. Books and papers were scattered over the floor, mingling with personal possessions and half-packed bags. The old man sat down rather gingerly on an unstained chair of white wood. He could find nowhere to put his hat; both the table and the iron bed were covered with various bits and pieces.

Cambus apologised for the mess. "I'm a very busy man," he said. Then he at once came to the point. "You've come at the right time, Devigny. I got a letter from your son yesterday, posted in Saint-Etienne."

"You mean he's got out?"

"I'm afraid not."

Cambus took down a book from the shelf by him, riffled through the pages, and took out two small yellow sheets of paper: the first letters I had passed on to Bury when I was in cell 45. These he put into the old, lined hand stretched out to receive them. The old man read them slowly, out loud, pausing after each phrase. Then he repeated part of what he had read:

"*I'm half-starved . . . don't forget my family . . . the condemned block . . .*"

Slowly he unfolded the second letter and read:

"*This message is meant for everyone—for you, for my parents, for my wife when she returns. Be sure that you pass it on. It is written by a prisoner who once thought only of his country, but now dwells on his wife, his children, his parents, all those for whom he feels love and affection. I have never been so close to you as I am now. Never before have I realised what a fine thing it is to belong to a family. I only appreciate all that I once had now I have lost it. Nothing can equal the affection of one's father or mother; nothing can replace the love of one's wife, the close ties of one's family. If all turns out well, how we shall prize those first days when we can once more live together in a free, happy France! I have confidence and hope. So must you. Do not let yourself be crushed by misfortune. Confidence is always the key to victory.*"

There was a long silence. A tear formed in the old man's eye, trickled down his withered cheek, and was lost in the whiteness of his beard.

"He thinks he's done for," he said at last. "For André to write that means that he's lost all hope."

Cambus, sympathising with the old man's grief, said nothing. From outside came the shouts of children leaving a class-room. Otherwise all was quiet.

"In our family," the old man said, "we don't make a habit of exposing our inner thoughts in that way. If André has broken the rule, it must mean that he's miserable and desperate. It reads like a will, a testament."

Cambus said: "He hasn't forgotten anybody. He's even tried to warn his Resistance friends. And don't forget that he ends his letter to you on a note of optimism."

"That's to stop us being worried. Have another look at the one he sent you. He's worrying about the future of his wife and children. I know him well enough to realise that he means this seriously. He's given up hope of ever seeing them again. And he's half-starved, he says. In my day we had a different idea of what war meant. It would have been a dishonourable act not to share our last crust with a prisoner.

"Let them shoot him if that's the law, but not let him die like an animal in some filthy dungeon. He's appealing for help, the poor boy. I shall go and see the German authorities. I remember in 1914 I gave two wounded Germans my water-bottle, and dragged them back out of no-man's-land. War without rules is no war. I'm not afraid. I shall go and see them. That's what I came for."

Cambus was at a loss for words. The old man's angry resolution had taken him aback. The poor devil, he thought; he doesn't know the Gestapo. If he lodges a protest, they'll throw him into prison as well as his son. There'll be two of them instead of one. I must stop him doing anything so stupid. The most important thing is to gain time.

"Monsieur Devigny," he said at length, "the first thing you

must do is to take your son a parcel. He says in his letter that they can be received on the fifteenth and thirtieth of each month. Today is the fourteenth. You can go tomorrow."

"I have some clothes and toilet materials for him in this parcel. I'll buy some food in a shop on the way to the prison."

"You won't find anything to buy. We're very badly off for food here in the town. Everything's on ration; you can't buy a penny-worth without producing a coupon for it. The best thing you can do is to go and see a friend of mine who's a butcher. His name is Plateau. He's got a shop in the Avenue de Saxe."

"If I'd known how things were," the old man said, "I could have brought some food myself, our own produce. It's getting late now. I'd better find myself a hotel room for the night."

"That's out of the question. Most of the hotels are requisitioned, and the rest shut. There isn't a single bed in Lyons. But I think I can help you. You can sleep here, and I'll stay with a friend of mine nearby. You won't need to fill in a registration form then, either."

"What registration form?"

"A form on which you have to fill in all your personal particulars. Hotel-keepers send them up to police headquarters every morning."

The old man said: "I haven't been here for thirty years, and I haven't slept away from home for at least twenty. I've lost the hang of these things."

"Don't worry. I'm here to see you don't get into trouble. Now we'd better go and see that butcher if your son's going to get anything to eat."

They left the house and walked back towards the river. The old man noticed that Cambus frequently glanced back over his shoulder.

Suddenly he stopped and said: "How did he get those two letters out of Montluc? And why were they posted in Saint-Etienne?"

"I haven't the faintest idea," Cambus said. "It's still worrying me."

They walked on towards the butcher's shop, each deep in thought.

The following day they set out from Cambus' apartment for Montluc. They had to walk right across the city, crossing the Saône by the same footbridge as the old man had used, and the Rhone by the Pont de la Guillotière. Cambus had insisted on accompanying Devigny. The old man hardly knew Lyons at all; and Cambus wanted, besides, to keep an eye on his behaviour in public. After a while they saw the chimneys of the tobacco factory in front of them.

"We're there," Cambus said, dully. It sounded as if he was afraid.

A tram from Perrache was slowly turning the bend by the bridge. They waited for it to pass, little knowing that three weeks earlier, in exactly the same spot, I had been the main actor in a quick, fierce tragedy which had nearly cost me my life.

"It's over there on the left, beyond the bridge," Cambus said. "I'll wait for you here."

The old man walked off, with his heavy, solid gait, a parcel in each hand. Cambus watched him. He stopped in the middle of the road and stared at Montluc Prison. He took in the central block at one glance, and then let his eye dwell on the third floor. The cells, with their tiny barred windows, were just visible above the high, grey walls. Cambus understood and shared his emotions.

The old man began walking again, more slowly now, with visible hesitation in his step. He turned to the left, stopped a cyclist, and asked where the main gate was. Then he turned right and skirted the outer wall, which cast its shadow over a large empty square. He stopped in front of an imposing iron door, and put his two parcels down on the cobbles. Then he looked up, as if trying to gauge the height of the wall. He hesitated for a moment, wiped his damp forehead with a handkerchief, and then pressed the bell. This was set at the normal height beside a second, smaller iron door, which had no handle.

He stood there waiting.

A small window opened in the wall on the right, and a soldier peered through the bars at the old man standing outside, a parcel in each hand.

"Who's it for?" he asked.

"Lieutenant Devigny," said the old man.

The window snapped shut, and then, after a moment or two was opened again. The soldier stared at the old man curiously. The door slid back on its metal rollers, and the old man went inside. He had hardly taken a step forward when he heard a sharp click behind him; the door had been shut again. He was a prisoner.

He found himself in a small yard. On his right was a small guard-house. Through a narrow barred window the soldier's face appeared.

The soldier opened the window and said: "Give up."

The old man passed over his two parcels, one after the other. "This one contains personal belongings," he said. "That one's food."

The German looked at him. "Open them."

He watched the old man's hands carefully as they struggled with the knots in the string, observing the whitened scars, the black lines with which they were seamed. Then he glanced at that ancient face, wrinkled with the toil of years; and undid the parcels himself.

He went through the personal effects quickly, without paying any particular attention to its contents, though these included a packet of razor-blades. Then he scribbled a number on it and pushed it aside. He whistled admiringly as he handled the fine sausages and sliced ham that the butcher had provided. He weighed the food in his hand, and put it in a different corner. This time he wrote nothing on the parcel.

The old man did not miss a thing.

"I would like to see my son," he said. His strong, unhurried voice echoed oddly in this iron-bound concrete cage.

"Impossible. Forbidden," the sentry said, and pulled a cord attached to a counterweight, which opened the sliding door outside.

The old man took one last look at the German and the inside of the prison, and went out without saying a word. The door rolled into place behind him.

He walked slowly round the prison walls, glancing up their vast height once or twice, passed the building which housed the Courts Martial Tribunal, crossed the road and stopped again on the railway bridge. He stood there for some time, watching these barred windows high up in the central block, indifferent to passers-by who elbowed him aside.

Cambus saw him there, woke him gently out of his preoccupied reverie, and led him away. He had some difficulty in stopping the old man from going to Gestapo headquarters, and convincing him that as things were he merely ran the risk of being arrested and confined in Montluc himself if he did what he proposed. He argued diplomatically, promised to do everything he could, agreed to find out how the case stood, and hinted that I might be able to get another letter out.

The old man reflected, thinking of the children left in his house. Finally he made an appointment with Cambus for the twenty-ninth, shook hands vigorously, and went back home.

Poor man, Cambus said to himself as he hurried down the steps to the station. I stopped him doing anything silly today, but he'll certainly try again next time.

The last tram from Annemasse had gone. There would not be another one till the following day. Resolutely the old man stepped out on the road, and got home five hours later, in the dark. It was pouring with rain.

My mother ran out to meet him. "I've seen him," he said. "He's all right."

A fortnight later, Cambus met the old man as arranged, at the station. He looked tired as he got out of the train. He had walked nearly twenty miles that morning to pick up a connection at Annemasse, and was carrying two packages. One of these was both bulky and heavy, the other somewhat smaller.

"Have you any news?" he asked at once.

Cambus shook his head. He did not dare admit that a second letter had, in fact, reached him, posted (like the first) in Saint-Etienne.

In this letter I wrote:

. . . I should be glad if you would tell Françoise's father [Colonel Groussard] that I rely on him to see that my family are provided for. Also, could you let them know from time to time that I'm doing all right? I don't want my parents and in-laws to get too worried through lack of news. Something will also have to be done, after the war, about getting my wife back to France. In this connection you might communicate with my parents. They live at Habère-Lullin, in Haute-Savoie.

Despite all my privations, my dear Jean, I keep in good spirits. God, and the knowledge that I have done my duty, help me to hold out.

Cambus said: "We'd better get off to Montluc before it's too late."

They walked away from the station in the direction of the prison. Cambus carried the big parcel; the string bit into his fingers. He left the old man at the corner of the wall, and waited for him near the bridge.

About a dozen people were waiting in front of the little iron door. The old man joined the queue behind an old lady who carried a small packet in each hand. There were men and women of all ages and conditions there, but more women than men. Some of them had brought their children with them, as if to draw additional comfort from their presence.

He could not fail to notice the anxiety and distress so clearly visible on every face. He was almost ashamed of the size of his parcels when he saw those the others were carrying. They can't get hold of anything in the town, he thought, and what there is must be terribly expensive.

The old lady smiled at him. She hesitated a moment, then said: "Got someone in there?"

"Yes. One of my sons. Have you?"

"My son and my husband."

"Have they been there long?"

"My son's been in three months. My husband was arrested a month later, when he went to complain to the Gestapo, and try and find out what was happening."

The old man's jaw tightened, and his moustache bristled. This always happened when he was angry or upset.

"Have you had any news?" he asked.

"No. All I know is that they're here, because the guards take in my parcels."

The young woman next to her joined in the discussion.

"My brother's been here for three weeks. We haven't had any news either."

"Can't they write letters?" the old man asked.

"No. It's not allowed. All we can do is bring in a parcel twice a month. You have to be careful what you put in them, too. No alcohol, no tobacco."

The guard asked each visitor their name in turn. One by one they were admitted through the sliding door, which promptly shut behind them. Each reappeared a few moments later, pale and downcast.

A pleasant young woman called out: "M. Brunoy."

The guard shut the window, opened it again a minute later, and called through the bars: "No Brunoy here."

"You're mistaken," the woman said. "He is here. He's my husband—"

"He's not here. Not any more."

The woman's eyes widened. She turned, dropped her parcel, and fainted.

The old woman whispered: "Her husband must have been transferred. Or shot. No one knows what goes on behind those walls. Look at that woman there, second in the queue. She comes every fortnight, waits for hours, and always has her parcel still when she goes away. Her boy's only eighteen. It's terrible."

The old man looked at the white-faced, silent woman; she was standing about four paces in front of him, and seemed to be praying.

He thought: Perhaps they'll take her parcel this time. She'd be so happy simply to know he was alive.

He was the last one admitted.

The guard was impressed by the size and contents of the big parcel. He examined all the articles it contained, made a pretence of hesitating over some of them, but finally passed the lot. The old man put the smaller one on the table.

"No, no. One, not two. Forbidden," the German said.

"It's for you," said the old man. He unpacked a bottle of home-made marc, some slices of ham, and a sausage. "Good stuff."

The guard uncorked the bottle, sniffed, looked at the food, and thanked him. Then he pulled the cord and the door rumbled open.

The old man went out. From the way he walked and muttered to himself, it was obvious that he was angry. He would have been more angry still if he had known that I would get little more than the big carton and the string that held it together.

Bury was a dominating, impulsive, plain-spoken man; uncompromising, yet extremely generous. He was convinced that he had a mission in life: to do all he could to free his country and restore the rule of law and order.

He and his family had been expelled from Alsace in 1940. With some difficulty he got himself the job of Chief Censor in Saint-Etienne, a position he rapidly lost. He then joined the *Tribune*, and had not been working on the paper more than a fortnight when he was arrested by the Gestapo, together with Blanchonnet, the editor, and Kuster, the local Chief of Police. He was indifferent to danger. It was all part of the game as far as he was concerned. He was incapable of remaining neutral, even in prison.

He had been forcibly conscripted into the German Army in 1915, and badly wounded a year later. He had spent the rest of the war in various hospitals. As a result he spoke German fluently, and was minutely acquainted with the workings of the German mind, both civil and military. He took advantage of this to outwit and gain the sympathy of his captors. Fränzel in particular had an instinctive respect for this former German officer, with his distinguished war record, and pitied his ill-luck in attracting the attentions of the Gestapo.

Bury spent some time explaining to Fränzel both the reasons for his arrest, and his personal attitude to Hitler. In the course of this discussion he realised that Fränzel himself had no reason to like the Hitler régime, and was very lukewarm about the war in general and the Russian campaign in particular. Fränzel made a sharp distinction between what he called "terrorists," those prisoners who, he claimed, had "stabbed German soldiers in the back," and the victims of the Gestapo, who found themselves imprisoned for beliefs which he largely shared himself. This explained his brutality to some prisoners, and the favours he showed to others.

This fact earned Bury himself certain advantages and privileges, of which both Kuster and Blanchonnet reaped the profit. All three, for example, were allowed to walk freely in the small courtyard beside the women's living-quarters. And—a unique privilege, this—Bury was allowed to see his daughter once a week.

A few days after his arrest, two men burst into his flat in Saint-Etienne and began to search it. They took no notice of Bury's wife and daughter, who were both present.

When they found nothing, they took the young girl aside, and told her that her father had been condemned to death.

She gasped, and then said: "But why?"

One of the Gestapo officers said: "There is only one way to save him. He has some secret documents hidden here or in the Censor's Office. Find them, and bring them to us."

It was an obvious trick, and she saw through it immediately. She decided to play up to them. She told them that she loved her father very much, and would do anything to save his life. She agreed to come to Gestapo headquarters and show them any documents she found, either in the flat or at her father's office.

To make her actions appear more plausible, the girl, in consultation with her mother, decided to do nothing for two days, and to conduct a feigned search in the Censorship Office in case she was being watched.

Two days later she went to the German police, looking very distressed, and told them she had found nothing. Her artless, irresponsible air was most convincing. She took advantage of the subject under discussion to ask where her father was.

At Lyons, they told her.

"He must be in Montluc, then," she said.

"That's right."

"Can you give me authority to take something to him in prison?"

"That isn't in our jurisdiction. You'll have to apply to our colleagues in Lyons."

"Who ought I to see?" the girl persisted. She knew very well that to gain admission to such a place she had to know the name of someone working there.

"Ask for M. Hermann at the Station Hotel," they said, laughing. They were convinced she would never get anywhere near him.

The following day, about two in the afternoon, she descended from a train at Lyons, clutching a parcel crammed with food, chocolate, cigarettes, and other supplies. She went down to the ladies' cloakroom, washed, and made up her face carefully. Her appearance had to be impeccable. She was dressed smartly, but not showily: a plain grey tailored costume, with pleated skirt, a little sailor-hat with a short veil, a blue-and-red scarf, and a brown handbag. Scared that she might lose her nerve, she decided to put her plan into action at once.

By mistake—and this mistake helped her considerably—she approached the hotel from the wrong side, and went through a side-entrance that opened on a quiet boulevard. In this way she avoided all the guards and form-filling. She found herself face to face with a lift-boy.

"I have an appointment with Herr Hermann," she said in German. "He is waiting for me. Kindly tell me his floor and room number."

"Fourth floor, the fourth door along."

She knocked. A man of about thirty, in uniform, stared at her in astonishment as she came in. She walked forward smiling.

"Herr Hermann?"

"That is my name."

"I have come to see you because my father has been arrested. Several weeks ago, in fact. He is detained in Montluc Prison. I saw your colleagues at Saint-Etienne, and one of them told me you were the only person who could give me the necessary authorisation to take him a parcel in prison."

"That is not in fact, true," the German said. "They made a mistake—"

She interrupted him.

"Look, I know what an influential person you are. The whole thing's very easy. You write me the authorisation, and I take the parcel to Montluc. There's nothing difficult about that, is there?"

She untied the parcel and spread out its varied contents on Hermann's desk.

"Cigarettes?" he exclaimed. "They're forbidden. And so is brandy."

"Of course. I realise that. I can understand your surprise. Such things are hard to get these days, I know. I was thinking of you, too. Please accept these cigarettes and chocolates—"

He said: "How did you get into my office?"

"Very easy. I walked in and said I wanted to see you."

He looked at her thoughtfully. Then he picked up his pen and wrote: *Permission is hereby granted to Mlle. Bury to leave a parcel in Montluc Prison for her father.* He signed this document, and banged a large official stamp on it.

"You are very kind," she said, and put it carefully away.

A little dazed, she found herself out in the street again. She asked a passer-by the way to Montluc.

"Montluc!" He looked quickly at the parcel, obviously guessing her errand. "Change at Avenue de Saxe."

She had to wait a long time for her second tram. To cheer herself up and soothe her nerves she bought some flowers at a shop opposite.

She got off at the railway bridge.

"On your right," intoned the conductor, "the tobacco factory; on your left—Montluc."

The road was deserted. After a moment's searching she found the little door and pressed the bell.

"Who are you? What do you want?" the guard shouted through his little window.

"I have a parcel for my father. This is a special permit from the Gestapo."

A hand stretched out and took the paper. The window was shut once more. She waited anxiously. At last the door opened, and she found herself shut in, facing a soldier behind a small grill.

"My father is here," she said. "This parcel is for him."

"Is your father a terrorist?" the soldier asked.

She laughed. "What an idea! No, he was taken as a hostage."

Another soldier came up and whispered for a moment. The sentry pulled a cord, and the inner door opened. She walked forward a little uneasily and found herself in the perimeter. Four or five soldiers gathered round her.

"Come on in," said one. "You'll be far better off here."

The sun was shining, and the heat between these high walls was considerable. On her right, under the lee of the sentries' post, she saw a bench and several cane chairs. As time went by she felt more and more nervous. Were they going to keep her here? The soldiers stood round her trying to make conversation. She began to chat with them. Then, suddenly, everything seemed to spin round in front of her eyes. Was she dreaming? No; it was her father, standing motionless there, a dozen paces away, with a stocky, bespectacled little warrant officer beside him.

She could not move.

The little man in glasses grinned.

"Aren't you going to kiss each other?" he said.

She flung herself into her father's arms. He said to the warrant officer: "This is my daughter."

She shook hands with Fränzel, who clicked his heels. The other soldiers had vanished.

Bury explained. "This gentleman is in command here. He is very kind to me. Very understanding."

Then, seeing the irritated expression on the Head Warder's face, he said to his daughter: "Please speak in German."

The subsequent conversation was conducted half in French, half in German; Bury's daughter had not made a habit of talking German with her father. She apologised for each mistake she made.

She gave him the flowers she had bought in the Avenue de Saxe. Fränzel watched, a little anxiously; then, convinced that all was well, he politely stepped out of earshot. This enabled them to talk more freely.

The girl quickly gave him all the family news, and passed on the latest developments at the front. She learnt that her father had been several times interrogated by Barbier, the head of the Lyons Gestapo, and would not be released. They talked for about ten minutes.

Fränzel at length interrupted them. He came up and said: "You must leave now. Someone might see you."

Bury took the hint. He said to his daughter, one eye on the warrant officer: "We have arranged for you to come back and bring me parcels. You can take away my dirty laundry, too."

Fränzel nodded. "Certainly. Come and see your father again. When you come, give your name and ask for me."

"When can I come?"

"Shall we say next Friday?"

She thanked him, astonished at such politeness. Fränzel said good-bye to her and walked away, nodding to Bury as he went. She flung herself into her father's arms once more. He looked at her affectionately, and quickly whispered a list of names of people who had been arrested in Saint-Etienne.

"Go and see their relations. Say that they are in good health and excellent spirits. Make sure everyone knows. Next time you come back I'll have some letters for you to deliver."

While he was talking he passed her a folded piece of paper from the inside pocket of his coat. She slipped it quickly down her dress.

"Give that to your mother," he said.

The transfer of this paper had taken only a fraction of a second.

They parted then, and Bury went away without looking back. His daughter, slightly bewildered, made for the exit. The door was shut, so she called a sentry.

"Was that your father?" he asked.

She nodded, choking, on the verge of tears.

"You poor kid. Don't worry. The war'll be over soon."

He pulled the cord, and the door slid open.

So, by a series of unlooked-for accidents, she was enabled to get into Montluc, see her father, and take letters out with her. After this she visited the prison once or twice a week. When she arrived she gave her name and asked the guard to tell his commanding officer that Monsieur Bury's daughter wanted to see him. On each occasion she was taken through the two sliding doors and waited for her father in the perimeter. When he came, he always had Fränzel with him.

The little warrant officer was invariably polite to her. He tried not to behave like a gaoler, and always refused any kind of payment for his trouble. Accordingly the young girl made a point of offering him chocolates or cakes. This delighted and touched him. It made him think of his own family, his daughter especially, who was about the same age as Bury's.

He also turned out to be very fond of flowers. The girl bought some before every visit, and gave him a few of them.

Bury always passed on letters to her at the end of their meeting, when Fränzel had retired to let them kiss each other goodbye. She took the bundle and hid it rapidly. (Sometimes she brought replies, and gave them to him the same way.) These letters were written on very odd material: lavatory paper, wrappings, even bits of cardboard from boxes.

At the end of one visit, in late April, her father seemed more agitated than usual.

"There's a new arrival," he whispered, "a Lieutenant Devigny. Condemned to death. They've half-killed him already. His messages must be posted tonight, without fail. It's very important. He's got to warn his friends."

That was how my letters, and those of many other prisoners in Montluc, reached the outer world.

At first Bury's daughter did not examine these letters, considering them purely private. She abandoned her scruples when she accidentally saw her own name in one of them. It was from a prisoner who wanted to use her as a messenger between him and his wife, so that they could keep up a regular correspondence. Through normal channels, what with postal censorship and the Gestapo, it would have been impossible. His wife would have almost certainly been arrested.

For safety's sake, Mlle. Bury kept all the mail to post in Saint-Etienne. If there was someone standing near the prison door when she arrived, she always went away and came back later. Once she noticed a black van standing a little way off. There was no one inside it. She went on to the door; but the guard told her in a scared voice that it was impossible for her to make her visit that day, as the Gestapo were in the prison. Another time (obviously the regular day for the delivery of family parcels) she came on quite a large queue. Patiently she strolled up and down, waiting for them to go.

Eventually the last visitor, an old man with a broad-brimmed hat, went off slowly, as if against his will. She could now present herself at the door. A quarter of an hour later she found the old man still standing on the bridge. He was staring at the prison. She was struck by his keen eyes, by the great white moustache that spread out across his face; but most by the air of deep misery which he conveyed.

They both walked to the tram-stop at the other side of the bridge. Here he found a tall, brown-faced man waiting for him. The two men sat down opposite her.

The old countryman said nothing. But his face was drawn and tense, his eyes full of distress.

After a moment, the younger man said: "Monsieur Devigny, we have to change trams twice to get to Plateau's shop."

The girl started as she heard this name; she knew that the man in front of her must be the lieutenant's father. She felt a wild urge to say: "Did you get those letters? I was the person who posted them. I may have another one on me now." Then she pulled herself together. I must remain silent, she thought, for his sake as much as mine. It would be a frightful risk to take. She sat there, forcing herself not to speak, consumed by her secret knowledge. She relaxed a little when the old man vented some of his ill-humour on the conductor, who refused to believe he was entitled to a reduced fare, despite the pass he carried.

Devigny's temper was all the more violent for having been so long held in. Over this tiny incident with the conductor he worked himself up to indiscriminate abuse of Lyons and all its inhabitants.

"You ought to come to Savoy, M. Cambus," he said at length. "Things don't change there. Savoyards know that old ways are the best."

Mlle. Bury thought: It's the prison he's really thinking about. He holds all these unknown people responsible for his son's detention.

She guessed that the old man's companion must be the schoolmaster who received and sent on the letters she posted in Saint-Etienne.

As he got off the tram, Cambus noticed the lingering glance of sympathy which the young girl opposite him gave Devigny. A few steps further on he stopped, and said in a low voice, as if he were talking to himself: "How do the letters get out of Montluc, and why are the posted in Saint-Etienne?"

Then the oddly assorted pair, one angry, the other thoughtful, went off together to find Plateau's shop.

In the months that followed, the old man made two more trips to Lyons. On each occasion, Cambus was faithfully waiting for him at their meeting-place. Devigny got into the habit of arriving the previous night; but so as not to put Cambus to any inconvenience, he said nothing about this, and spent the night on a bench in the station waiting-room. On the return journey he invariably got to Annemasse too late to catch the last tram, and proceeded to walk home—a matter of nearly twenty miles.

One day late in June, Cambus realised as soon as he saw the old man, that something was wrong.

He relieved him of his parcel. "I must say, you've certainly tied this up well," he said.

"That was what my son wanted. He said he wanted some strong linen shirts, too, as well as food."

"*What?*"

"A prisoner who had been released from Montluc came to see me at home. He gave me a letter from André. André said in this letter that he wanted some linen shirts, and would I please use long, tough pieces of string to tie up my parcels in future? That's all."

"Ah," said Cambus, a little puzzled now.

"This business can't go on any longer," the old man said. "I know what kind of a life he's leading in there now. I've made up my mind to go and see the Gestapo chief, today."

This time, Cambus thought, there's no point in arguing. He's going to do it. He must have been thinking it over for days. His mind's made up.

"Is this France or isn't it? I'm going to see Colonel Barbier presently, and tell him what I think. In the meantime, we'd better take this parcel to the prison."

And once again he produced a second, smaller parcel for the guard. The German sniffed the bottle of marc, took a long swallow from it, and then handed it back to the old man.

"Keep it," he said. "You need it more than I do."

The old man left the prison even crosser than usual.

"That's the last straw," he grumbled to himself. "Accepting a present from a Boche!"

That day, by some lucky chance, the conductor allowed him his reduced fare.

It was a quarter to twelve when Cambus left him in the middle

of the town. They arranged to meet at one, in a café in the Rue du
Bélier. Cambus warned him to be careful, and (to be on the safe
side) gave him a second, emergency rendezvous for two o'clock at
the tram-stop. It was with deep feeling that he watched the old
man walk off, firm and self-assured, in the direction of Gestapo
headquarters. He was carrying his walking-stick and knapsack.

Poor bastard, he thought. To save his son he's walking straight
into the lion's mouth.

The old man climbed the station steps and boldly marched up
to the main entrance of the hotel. He went through the revolving
door and at once came up against a sentry, who pounced on him
with the intention of removing his stick and bag. The old man
firmly brushed him aside and said, in his strong, clear voice: "I have
come to see the Colonel."

The sentry (who had not understood a word) was about to return to the attack and carry out his standing orders, when an officer
in uniform appeared.

"Who are you?" he asked the old man. "What do you want?"
He spoke French without a trace of accent.

"My name is Devigny. I am a landowner from Habère-Lullin,
and I have come to see the Colonel."

"Why?"

"I have something important to discuss with him."

The officer was intrigued. "Wait here till I come back," he said.
He disappeared. (He was, in fact, Major Timann, who had dealt
with my case.) The old man sat down. The sentry could do nothing, but continued to stare fiercely at him. A few minutes later the
officer reappeared.

"Follow me," he said.

They went up together in the lift.

Timann stared at the old man. The old man returned his stare.

Timann thought: The son is like the father.

The old old man thought: He looks a real Boche.

Fourth floor. They went through a guarded steel door, turned
right, and entered a large room. Timann knocked at an inner door,

and ushered the old man into the presence of Colonel Barbier, chief of the Gestapo in Lyons. Then he withdrew, shutting the door, and left them alone together.

Barbier examined the old man from behind his desk.

"What do you want?" he asked.

"My son has been imprisoned in Montluc for four months. He's done nothing." The old man's authoritative voice startled the German. "I have come to ask when you propose to release him."

Barbier made no reply. He looked at his visitor for some little time, noting the sparse white hair, the fearless blue eyes, the deep wrinkles that furrowed his skin, and the heavy upturned moustache. His bearing was proudly independent, his clothes worn but good. He wore studded boots, and carried a black hat in one hand. He had a flower in his button-hole, a knapsack slung from one shoulder, and leant on a heavy walking-stick.

At last Barbier said: "Sit down, please."

The old man sat down in a large leather armchair. He put his hat on his knees and rested his stick between his legs.

"Were you in the last war?" Barbier asked.

"I did my duty, Colonel, as you are doing yours. I fought for my country."

"In what arm?"

"An infantry regiment."

Barbier pressed a button. An N.C.O. appeared, and Barbier gave him some orders in German. He came back almost at once, put a dossier on the desk, and went out again.

The old man stared at the cardboard file, bulging with papers, and wondered what was in it. To put a good face on matters he went on: "We haven't had any news. We don't know what's happening. And then someone advised me not to come here. I told them I was going to see the Colonel, that I wasn't afraid. Just now, downstairs, I said the same thing. 'It's the chief I want to see,' I said, 'the Colonel, no one else will do.' Colonel, I rescued two wounded German soldiers in 1914. Am I likely to be afraid now?"

While he listened to this, Barbier had the dossier open and was flipping through the contents. The old man saw his features grow hard and angry. Occasionally Barbier glanced up at him. If only I knew what that young devil André had been up to, he thought.

The Colonel said, abruptly and brutally: "Your son! Your son was a terrorist. He was working for the British Intelligence Service."

He spoke the words "Intelligence Service" in English, carefully spacing out the syllables.

"What is this 'Intelligence Service'?"

Barbier said, as if addressing a child: "The British—official—espionage—organisation. Understand?"

The old man was shocked. He understood. "No, no, it's out of the question," he said in some agitation. "I know my son, he understands what honour means as well as I do. He's a brave regimental officer, like a lot of your fellows—all for a good hard scrap. He'd never do anything underhand, though. I brought him up, and I can answer for him."

"We have proof of his activities—here, in this dossier."

"I don't believe it. Colonel, I raised seven children up there in the mountains. I taught them two things—to enjoy hard work, and behave decently. My son could never do a thing like that."

Barbier said: "Children can be brought up the right way, and still go to the bad."

"Have you any children yourself?" the old man asked.

"Yes, four."

"In that case, Colonel, I'm sure that if you were in my shoes you'd do what I'm doing now. You get fond of these kids, you sacrifice yourself to educate them and get them decent jobs. You've got to think of their mother, too . . ."

He rambled on, convinced that Barbier could not fail to be moved by this argument. But Barbier was in fact treating the old man as a potential source of information, who might unwittingly put the last touches to his son's dossier. He said: "If your son had confessed, we might have done something for him."

"How can he confess when he hasn't done anything? And how do you think he can defend himself when he's shut up in prison? We can't even write to him."

Barbier said: "That's easily remedied. You can write to him now. Tell him that if he confesses he'll be released."

He produced a pen and began hunting for a sheet of paper. Frowning, the old man watched every move he made, determined to get behind the impassive mask that the Colonel presented to him. He smelt a trap somewhere.

He said: "My wife's written the letters in our house for the last forty years. Women know what to say to children better than we do. Besides, I can't write now." He stretched out his crippled hand for Barbier's inspection. "I got that from a piece of shrapnel. Gerbvillier, 1914."

"Where did you spend last night?"

"On a bench in the station waiting-room. I left home yesterday. I had to walk twenty miles to catch my train, and I shall have to walk twenty miles back tonight. I don't mind about that. I was determined to have a personal interview with you, Colonel, and now I have."

Barbier took another look at the old man's studded boots, the flower in his button-hole, his withered hand. He found himself admiring the pride and assurance which animated that weatherbeaten face.

He got up, and the old man did likewise.

He came round the desk and said: "Unfortunately I can do nothing to help you. But despite what I have told you, you should be proud of your son."

The old man's moustache bristled with emotion. He fiddled with his knapsack, trying to gain time, searching for something else to say. The Gestapo officer walked past him and opened the door.

Outside in the corridor the old man said: "Is he well cared for in prison? Surely you can tell me that? Have you put him in a communal barracks where he can talk to other prisoners? I can't bear to think of him in solitary confinement."

"Don't worry. We'll see to that." Timann was waiting outside the door, and Barbier whispered a few words in his ear. Then he said good-bye to the old man and went back into his office.

The major followed him as far as the landing.

The old man had been scared by the whispered conversation between Barbier and Timann; he began to wonder if he would be allowed out of the building.

Timann said something in German to the lift-boy.

They're going to arrest me downstairs, the old man thought.

When he reached the ground floor he made straight for the exit. He did not hurry, but carefully avoided looking at anyone. He hitched his knapsack over one shoulder, put on his hat, and went out into the street.

He felt a wild urge to walk quickly, even to enlist the services of one of those taxi-cyclists he had previously dismissed with contempt. He wanted to get into the little trailer and tell them to take him away, anywhere to get away. He controlled the impulse, however, and walked slowly down the steps without looking back.

Cambus had not left the tram terminus. From this position he had a good view of the hotel entrance. He saw the old man come out, heaved a vast sigh of relief, and followed him at a discreet distance. The old man walked uneasily now, and his stick tapped the ground with less than its usual assurance. Cambus had no difficulty, after a while, in catching up with him. It was a good thing I kept an eye on him, he thought. He never even looked back to see if he was being followed.

"Ah, there you are," the old man said, as Cambus drew level with him. He stopped, wiped away a tear, and then said to his companion, as if thinking aloud: "I don't mind him fighting for the English; but he was a fool to get caught."

He walked on a little, and then added: "He won't be so badly off now, though. Colonel Barbier promised me that he'd be put in a communal barracks."

Cambus slipped his arm through that of the old man, and they quickened their step. It was beginning to rain. Soon their figures faded and vanished behind a grey curtain of water.

9

The second rope could not be made till the very last moment. I had to use my mattress-cover in its construction, and I could not leave a heap of straw in my cell and all my equipment exposed to view.

To avoid losing time when this last job came to be done, I measured the width of the cover, and marked it out with my pencil in suitably broad strips.

Early in July I received a parcel. When I compared the size of the box with what was actually in it, I had no doubt that the guards had filched most of the contents. But they had left me two linen shirts, and about six yards of string were still wound round the parcel itself.

Excellent, I thought. I cut one of the shirts into narrow strips, which I used to make a section of thin, tough, pliable rope. I checked its length carefully, and hid it away. The second shirt I used to reinforce one end of the rope which was already prepared; the end, that is, that would pass over the sharp edge of the roof, and take a particularly heavy strain. I accordingly lagged about four feet of it with several thicknesses of cloth.

Most of my preparations were now complete, and only a few details remained to be cleared up. I strengthened the loops attached to the grappling-irons, and also the wire which bound the heaviest grappling-iron (the double one) to its rope. From time to time, when all was quiet in the corridor, and especially during the guards' mealtimes, I took all my equipment out; I got much satisfaction simply from looking at it and handling it. When night fell I added a little more rope to what I already possessed. It could, I am convinced, have taken ten times my weight.

Jeantet was still giving me little bits of advice.

"When you're climbing up you want all the purchase you can get. Plant your feet firmly against the wall. That way you'll be able to exert the full strength of your legs and arms."

He also suggested that I take a spare rope. If the one with which I was to cross the perimeter broke, there would be no sense in my beating my head hopelessly against the second wall for want of a way to scale it. I had politely refused the rope he had made from his bolster-case; I should probably have had to do the work all over again, and this seemed an unnecessary risk. He was somewhat put out at first by my refusal, but soon calmed down when I explained my reasons to him.

I also had to cut my hair and shave off my beard. By now they were as thick as a bush; I could hardly run around the countryside looking like a prehistoric monster. I made a razor by fixing one of my blades in a piece of split wood. With my chisel I cut a slit through the wood, and pushed the razor-blade into it. The cutting edge just projected on either side; if I held the wood tightly, the blade would stay firm. It was with this primitive instrument that, when the time came, I cut off my hair and beard and gave myself the appearance of a (more or less) normal human being.

At the same time I knew that a description of me would be circulated to every police-station in France if I succeeded in escaping. To change my appearance I decided to keep a large moustache. I may add that in prison one's skin becomes astonishingly hard. The whole operation was agony, and my razor-blades were blunted with cutting blankets. But I gritted my teeth and stuck it out.

Towards the end of July a nasty incident took place which disturbed us all and scared me in particular. At the time, I thought the game was up.

The midday meal had passed off as usual. To kill time I was holding a flea-race. This was one of my favourite amusements. I would put several of these horrible insects inside a small circle I had pencilled on the floor, and kept them there with a piece of paper. When I gave them a push with the paper, they scattered in all directions. The first to reach the outer circle were killed at once; they were obviously far too lively. The others, as a kind of consolation-prize, were reprieved for the time being.

Jeantet was stretched out on his bed; Grimaud was playing an endless game of knucklebones with two pebbles; Duflot, across the way, was scribbling something on his wall. The rest were tapping out messages, praying, or simply asleep.

Suddenly we heard loud shouts down on the ground floor, followed by a fusillade of shots. Iron-shod feet stamped up the stairs, doors were flung open. I went to my spy-hole and listened intently. Yes; they were approaching our floor. I threw a quick glance round to see that all was in order, and stood there, waiting. The key turned sharply in the door.

"Come on, outside. Look sharp!"

As I went out I saw the duty sergeant passing along the cells on the opposite side, and my companions looking questioningly at each other. Steel-helmeted soldiers, carrying guns, formed up on the landing and hurried us down the staircase. This time there was no attempt to make us keep the proper distance from each other.

I was behind Jeantet. He remained extraordinarily calm, merely looking over his shoulder and observing with sad resignation: "Too late!"

One look at those frightened faces was enough. The mass of men struggled through the door; an occasional shout could be heard as someone was kicked or slapped. The gleaming sub-machine guns that the guards carried told their own story. We were all, I was convinced, going to be shot there and then.

From every floor the prisoners streamed out into the big courtyard. Here, several men in plain clothes were waiting. They carried pistols. Several faces I had not seen for weeks were there, among them Nathan, who stood head and shoulders above everyone else.

It was a horrible sight. All these men, young and old, rich and poor, guilty and innocent alike were suddenly faced with the prospect of immediate death. Those pale, nervous, frightened faces formed a picture which will remain in my memory for a very long time.

Fifty; a hundred; soon the whole prison was there.

One of the civilians told us, in German, to fall in on parade. Most of us did not understand him. It took the cursing guards some time to get us drawn up.

The civilian called for an interpreter, and one of the prisoners, a tall, elderly man, stepped forward.

The civilian said: "One of you has smuggled a letter out in some dirty laundry. He has been caught and shot." So we had a Gestapo officer to deal with. He went on: "No more parcels will be allowed. Immediately after this parade there will be a collection of pencils from your cells. If you do not give them up, you will be shot, too. We shall search your belongings. The possession of pencils is forbidden."

The interpreter translated this speech phrase by phrase, in a powerful and surprisingly authoritative voice. When it was over someone raised his hand, presumably wanting to ask a question or make a protest. I could not hear what he said; but I saw the civilian walk up to him and drive his clenched fist into his face.

I'm done for, I thought, as I climbed the stairs to my cell with the others. If they make a search they'll find all my equipment.

"Are you going to hand over your pencil?" de Pury asked me.

"It might be wiser," I said.

The cells were locked again. I sat down and thought carefully.

No. That pencil was too precious. What was one more risk now? And I pushed it up the air-hole above the earth-closet.

Later that afternoon the duty sergeant came in.

"I haven't got a pencil," I told him.

He seemed cheerful and relaxed; obviously the Gestapo had left the prison.

The next day, during exercise, I asked de Pury if he had surrendered his pencil.

"No. Have you?"

I said I had kept mine, too.

I was, I realised, at the mercy not only of my own unconsidered actions, but those of my captors as well. But the pencil episode, though it disturbed me for a few hours, did not induce me to alter my plans. I still had to tell de Pury what I intended to do. He could give my family some information if I lost my life; and I wanted to ask him to intercede with God on my behalf, and ask forgiveness for my sins.

In any case I had to wait till the moon had waned; the nights were extraordinarily clear.

This delay was madness, nevertheless. Not only was my cell liable to be searched, but I ran the risk of being moved to another part of the prison. I might suddenly be condemned and executed; anything might happen.

On the morning of my hundredth day in Montluc I called out to the duty sergeant when he opened my door for morning exercise.

"Come here," I said.

He took a step forward, the bunch of keys dangling from his hand. I pointed at the tally of days on the wall.

"One hundred," I said. "*Hundert.*"

Then I offered him the thousand-franc note Nathan had given me, and explained in dumb-show that I wanted some cigarettes. He took the money, looked at me queerly, and went on to the next cell. It was a frightful risk to take, and all the more idiotic because I had no especial craving to smoke. Besides, I would lose the money, and it would have been invaluable to me outside. I at once regretted my involuntary gesture. It might even result in my clothes and cell being searched.

I would, I saw, have to repress my natural instincts, and muster all my will-power to prevent myself deviating in the slightest degree from the strict self-imposed code I followed. To my captors I must always appear a model prisoner, never giving any trouble, content with prison life, my only aim being to earn, by exemplary conduct, forgiveness for the criminal folly which had incited me to attempt escape.

That evening the duty sergeant brought me a packet of cheap cigarettes and some matches, but no change. This unexpected amiability relieved and disturbed me simultaneously. I had a wildly fantastic vision of the prison staff, moved to tears by my hundred days' captivity, shifting me to a public block or a more comfortable cell. Catastrophe!

But of course it was all moonshine, completely out of the question. I remembered Fränzel's face in the blacksmith's shop, beating me as I lay over the anvil, spitting in my face. The duty sergeant would not have told anyone else about his little errand; he wanted to keep the rest of the money.

Duflot, unlike me, really was a cigarette-addict. He had indicated as much to me many times, raising two fingers to his lips in frustrated pantomime, and to be cut off from tobacco altogether nearly drove him mad.

That night I went out of my cell, scratched gently at his door, and passed a few cigarettes and matches to him through the spyhole. Muffled exclamations of surprise and delight reached me from the depths of his cell.

When we went out the following morning, Duflot was preceded into the corridor by clouds of stale smoke, much to the astonishment of the guard. Duflot grinned at him. Another rash gesture on my part; but I was more than compensated for it by Duflot's evident pleasure. I gave the rest of the packet to Jeantet.

Duflot, for some reason I never found out, was shortly afterwards moved from his corner cell to a more comfortable one at the other end of the corridor. From the fanlight of his new quarters he could look down into a window in the corner of the courtyard, which belonged to a cell occupied by a woman. The first time he saw her wandering round stark naked, Duflot (as he told me himself) was scared out of his wits, and hastily retreated from the fanlight. Later he changed his attitude, and spent long periods watching her. They even exchanged a few words.

This woman must have been able to pull strings in some way or other, because on several occasions she got him a double ration of soup. One day a member of the fatigue-party produced a slice of bread for him, with a large pat of butter on it. Then, thinking better of such generosity, he grabbed it out of Duflot's hands, licked off the butter, and gave him back the bread.

The cell opposite mine remained empty: I missed Duflot's cheerful face. He had been useful to me, too; once when I had reassembled my door rather hastily, and some gaps showed between the boards, he spotted it from his spy-hole, and warned me in time.

Transfers to Fresnes and Compiègne were fairly frequent; but the vacant cells were rapidly filled by an ever-increasing number of new arrivals. The wooden barrack-hut and the old workshop opposite it were overflowing: the former with Jews, the latter with young delinquents or minor offenders. The courtyard was reserved for their use, and in the mornings we could now only use the area in front of the main entrance to the block. The groups were reduced to five or six, so that our outings only lasted a few moments. We emptied our buckets, went in twos or threes to the wash-house by the kitchen, then returned immediately to our cells. This made it easier for the German guard to keep a strict eye on us, and it was virtually impossible to talk. Discipline became more severe, and it was extremely difficult to make contact with our friends.

"What are you waiting for?" Jeantet asked me one day through his fanlight. "You're all ready. They may change your cell, or transfer you. The longer you wait, the less chance you have of success."

"I've still got something I must do, Eugene. I want to ask de Pury to help me make my peace with God. I need God's forgiveness to enable me to face death fearlessly. Perhaps the enforced penance I have undergone in this place is enough to wipe out my score. I don't know. I may even have something on the credit side. But it does no harm to be doubly sure."

I had to admit to myself, also, that the execution which I had carried out in Nice still weighed heavily on my conscience. I had killed a man who wore no uniform, in conditions which, reconsidered in solitude, appeared little less than barbaric. Angrisani's agonised face often troubled my dreams.

The profession of arms is, I know, entirely directed to one main end—the destruction of the enemy; but certain basic rules exist which transform war into a species of sport. The unorthodox methods I had employed made me feel I had broken these rules. This disturbed my peace of mind.

De Pury knew all about my plan to escape. He was aware that I had made a rope and dismantled my door. I tried, in the few moments at our disposal in the wash-house, to explain something of my sense of guilt. But it was almost impossible to talk seriously there. Accordingly I wrote him a letter, which I slipped into the pocket of his pyjama-top. This garment (like the rest of our clothes) was hung on the wire-netting of a hen-run behind the kitchens while we washed ourselves.

I got a bad scare when I saw Fränzel saunter up to the hen-run and begin poking about in various pockets; but on this occasion God must have been watching over me. Certainly Fränzel never found my letter.

The next day, de Pury passed me a sheet of paper on which he had copied out a passage from St. Luke:

> And it came to pass, that, as he was praying in a certain place, when he ceased, one of his disciples said unto him, "Lord, teach us to pray, as John also taught his disciples." . . . And he said unto them, "Which of you shall have a friend, and shall go unto him at midnight, and say unto him, 'Friend, lend me three loaves, for a friend of mine in his journey is come to me, and I have nothing to set before him?' And he from within shall answer and say, 'Trouble me not: the door is now shut, and my children are with me in bed; I cannot rise and give thee.' I say unto you, Though he will not rise and give him, because he is his friend, yet because of his importunity he will rise and give him as many as he needeth. And I say unto you, Ask, and it shall be given you; seek, and ye shall find; knock, and it shall opened unto you. For everyone that asketh, receiveth; and he that seeketh findeth; and to him that knocketh it shall be opened."

De Pury said: "Read this earnestly, and reflect on it."

When I was a child I said my prayers (whether in church or at home) in a mechanical way, thinking about something quite different.

In a prison cell, alone with my conscience and face to face with death, it was a different matter. Through the mediation of this passage from the Gospels, I approached God in a spirit of such sincere faith that the Almighty could not remain insensible to my appeal.

"I am happy now," I said to Eugene. "I have made my peace with God."

"How is that?"

"De Pury gave me a prayer to say."

He was silent for a moment, then asked me if I could give it to him.

I said I would slide it under his door that night. "But God will not listen to you unless you have faith in Him."

Yet God was to put me to the proof in such terrible circumstances, and make me pass through so agonising a Gethsemane, that I have often wondered whether He was, in fact, on my side.

De Pury not only set my conscience at rest, but soothed my mind considerably on the subject of my family.

My worst fear was that I might join the vast legion of the anonymous dead. Death in itself I could accept; but I wanted my relatives to know that I had fought to the end, without relaxing or giving up.

There are many kinds of death, both fine and ignoble. I at least wanted my end to reflect the pattern of my life; I wanted to die facing the enemy, so that my children would know that their father had never lost heart or surrendered. That was why I asked de Pury to tell them everything if the need arose.

Though he had never learnt how I opened the panel in my door, de Pury took my plan very seriously, and I told him as much about it as I could. Grimaud, on the other hand, remained unconvinced.

"It's impossible," he said to me in the wash-house.

"That," I said, "is precisely why I'm going to have a shot at it."

He looked at me pityingly. I was sure he thought me out of my mind.

Jeantet never tired of asking me why I was still delaying. "Hesitation means retreat," he informed me.

Unfortunately what he said was only too true. I knew very well that time was working against me. I had to make up my mind; and that was the last and hardest struggle of all. I had to overcome my inertia and acceptance of routine, swallow my fear and say *En avant!* —those two tiny, terrible words that hurl you into the fiery furnace in a split second of time.

August was passing, and the fatal words still stuck in my throat.

"What are you waiting for?" Eugene asked.

De Pury asked me several times what day I had decided on.

Grimaud thought: He'll never do it.

I called up all my reserves of courage and determination; I searched the depths of my being for the energy necessary to convert my dream into fact. But it was useless. The days went by, and I made no move.

On August 20 an unexpected development gave me the incentive I had hitherto lacked, and finally spurred me into action. After lunch the S.S. N.C.O. who had escorted me at the time of my first attempted escape came to take me away. As soon as I was out of my cell he handcuffed me. Then we made our way along the corridor and down the stairs.

Oh God, I thought, why did I wait so long? Why didn't I take Eugene's advice? Too late, too late . . .

Even before we were outside the front door, my escort had ostentatiously drawn his pistol; clearly he wanted to remind me that he had not forgotten our previous trip together.

Fränzel was in the courtyard. As I passed by he told me, in a threatening voice, not to get up to any tricks.

The car was drawn up by the curb, outside the main gate. I got in, and at once perceived that the doors had been locked. There was no chance of repeating my April escapade, especially since the S.S. man, pistol covering me and finger on the trigger, was watching the least move I made.

We turned left beyond the bridge, and followed the line of the railway. Then we turned down the Avenue Berthelot and pulled up outside the Public Health Department, which was the Gestapo's new headquarters.

What was going to happen? What did they want with me after so many weeks?

My heart was thudding with fear, and perspiration pricked out on my forehead. The S.S. escort had one hand on my sleeve and the other pressing the pistol into the small of my back. He pushed me along several corridors and up a flight of stairs. Finally we reached an office. There were three men in it. Major Ellers I recognised; beside him, seated behind a large desk, were two officers I had never seen before.

One of them (who was in fact, Colonel Barbier, the Gestapo chief) said: "The investigation of your case is complete. You will now pay the penalty for your activities against our German soldiers. You are to be shot. Both your espionage and your attempt to escape from captivity render you liable to death."

He spoke very clearly and precisely, spacing out each syllable. He watched me carefully all the time. I shivered, but I retained the strength to meet his gaze, and continued to stand rigidly at attention despite my trembling knees.

"You have sentenced me without allowing me to defend myself," I said.

"We have your dossier. That is enough. If you had confessed, perhaps . . ." He shrugged.

My clothes were tattered and threadbare, my whole body was grimy with prison filth, there were handcuffs on my wrists and I had spent four months in the cells; yet, confronted with these German officers, impeccable in their gleaming uniforms, I felt a great upsurge of strength. I was filled with pride: I had held out to the end, I had not weakened. Death was infinitely preferable to capitulation. I stood very straight, teeth clenched, and looked at each of them in turn. Then the S.S. guard dragged me away by main force.

In the corridor I stopped dead, ignoring his attempts to shove me on, and stared at him with such devouring hatred that he was startled into silence. I walked on in my own good time, and had taken a dozen paces at least before he began to curse at me again.

Why had I been sentenced in these peculiar circumstances?

What had been going on since April 17, the day of my arrest outside Annemasse station? Presumably our organisation had continued to operate, and the Germans were revenging themselves on such members of it as had fallen into their hands. Or perhaps there was simply a shortage of cells in Montluc. Or were they hoping to extort a confession from me by this threat of execution?

But on the way back to the prison one thought only occupied my mind: would I go back to the same cell?

All other preoccupations faded before this single obsessional fear. It seemed all too likely that, as in April, I should be transferred to the condemned block pending execution.

We returned by a different route. The banks of the Rhone flashed past. A few couples were strolling slowly along under the shade of the trees. Life went on its way like the river itself, changeless, indifferent, unfeeling. I would leave the world of people and become a mere *thing*, a corpse. A shiver ran through me.

The car crossed the railway bridge and pulled up with a scream of brakes outside the prison.

Each step I took in this chill, yet familiar building, every flight of stairs I climbed, I felt my confidence blossom out and return more strongly. I looked almost with affection at the walls of my prison, knowing that they harboured the means to save me. Like a miser crooning over his gold, I probed my mattress, took out the rope and the grappling-irons, and fondled them lovingly. They represented so many days of hope, patience and ingenuity, such a sum of anxiety and fear; and I had so nearly lost them all! But I had come back. Half-weeping, I knelt down against the wall and thanked God for this reprieve. There was still a chance.

There was not a moment to be lost. I would get to work on the second rope the minute the evening meal was over. Then a quick farewell to Eugene, and away to the roof and walls that were waiting for me.

Jeantet tapped several times. I answered, and was about to climb up to the fanlight when I heard footsteps in the corridor. I held my breath as they drew closer to my cell.

10

At the sound of the key turning in the lock I got to my feet. To my astonishment a young man walked into the cell. I saw Fränzel behind him. Fränzel's presence, and the new arrival's odd appearance and dress so flabbergasted me that I stood motionless beside my bed, completely at a loss.

When Fränzel had gone (without a word of explanation) and we were alone, I said, uncertainly, "*Du bist Deutsch?*"

He looked puzzled.

"Are you French?"

"Certainly," he said.

"What's your name?"

"Gimenez."

We shook hands.

This unexpected end to a highly dramatic day completely bereft me of coherent thought. It meant that all my plans were upset; but it also offered me companionship, the chance for free and uninterrupted conversation.

I had to make a tremendous effort to behave naturally. I don't know whether I succeeded in this at first; Gimenez turned very pale, and stared at me out of huge frightened eyes. His appearance was quite extraordinary. I had never seen either a French or a German soldier got up in quite this way.

His tunic and forage-cap were German Air Force issue, but his trousers and anklets equally certainly had come from the French Army. He looked like nothing so much as a P.O.W. who had tried to escape disguised as an enemy soldier, but had only managed to get hold of half the uniform.

The total effect was at once comical and uncouth. He was miserable, uncertain and worried; yet there was a shifty look in his eye. He was very pale, and his hair was long and filthy. He was hardly more than a boy. I didn't know what to make of him.

At last I said: "Haven't you got a bag or anything?"

He shook his head.

"Will you be in here long?"

"I don't know," he said. "This is the first place they've sent me to. I was arrested, and—"

I said: "There's only one mattress and two blankets. You sleep on the bed, and I'll try the floor. There's not much room, I'm afraid—"

"Have you been here long?" he asked.

"Look here, on the wall. Each stroke stands for a day. The crosses are Sundays. Here are the months. April, May, June, July. It's August 20 today. That means I've been here a hundred and twenty-five days. Since April 17, in fact."

I ran my finger over the calendar, talking on, fascinated by the sound of a voice in this cramped and silent place.

"A hundred and twenty-five days. Seventeen Sundays. It's been a long time. But now you're here it'll pass much faster. Look, that's the slop-bucket. Every morning when you go out to the courtyard you have to rinse it out with a little water and disinfect it with chlorate of lime. Here's an old jam-jar I managed to get hold of; I fill it with water during morning exercise and drink it on the way back. My personal belongings are in this box. Nothing much—a shirt, two handkerchiefs and a towel. These are all my possessions. Oh, I'm forgetting my razor. You wait. It's something out of this world. At first I tried to shave with a bare blade, but I couldn't hold it firm, it was always slipping on my beard. Now I've fixed it in a piece of wood, and tied it up with string. I cut my hair, too."

"By yourself?" he asked, apparently unmoved by this spate of words.

"Of course. I've got a tiny mirror. You'll see, it's easy to make yourself at home. It's a bit tough the first few days—there's not much air, for one thing—but you're lucky, you've got an old hand to help you. You won't have so bad a time of it as I did at first, in 13 and 45."

"You've changed cells, then?"

"Twice," I told him. "But I've been in this one over two months. It's well-situated and clean, and I get a bit of sun. Oh, be careful when you lie down; that bedstead's very fragile."

He said: "You have the bed. I'm used to floors; I've been sleeping in train-corridors recently."

"All right, if you insist. Anyway, the bed's just as hard as the floor. Tomorrow you can ask for a bed to yourself. I've seen prisoners two to a cell here before—they had a mattress each, so why shouldn't we?"

"Surely I could get it right away?"

"How?" I asked, amused.

"I could hammer on the door."

"Impossible. All you'd get would be a thick ear for making a noise. Tomorrow morning will be soon enough, when the duty sergeant comes to let us out."

There was a pause. I said: "Sit on the bucket, it's the most comfortable thing in the cell. We'll get some soup soon." I sat down myself, facing him, with my back against the wall.

"That's a nice pullover you've got," I said. "French Army issue, isn't it? I had one myself. Those are Army trousers too, I see."

"The Germans dressed me up in this lot at Versailles."

"The anklets will come in very handy. You'd better keep them on if you don't care for fleas: those little bastards get in everywhere."

He said: "I've never seen any fleas."

"No? Well, I'll show you some."

I lifted the corner of the bedstead and dropped it smartly. A few huge red fleas and a swarm of smaller white ones went scattering in all directions. I crushed some of them with my boot. I said: "They come out and attack us at night. The really smart ones climb up to the ceiling and drop on us from a great height."

He looked nervous. "There's an awful lot of them."

"Hundreds, probably thousands. They're everywhere. They run over your skin. It's unpleasant at first, but you get used to it. I even began to get fond of them. I've spent days studying their habits. I even play little games with them. They've been the only companions I've had. Look, I'll catch you one—"

"No, please don't, later perhaps—"

"As you prefer."

Another silence. I asked him when he had been arrested.

"This afternoon, by the French police."

"The *French* police?"

"Yes. You see, I was with a friend of mine on Tilsitt Bridge— we'd had a bit too much to drink, and we were pretending to shoot up the passers-by—just scaring them, you know. Then a French policeman turned up, and I really took a pot-shot at him, and unfortunately I hit him. Then a whole squad of them appeared, and we were arrested and carted off to the Gestapo."

"Is your friend in here with you?"

"They brought us here together. He must be in a cell somewhere near."

I asked him if he had killed the policeman, and he said he didn't know.

"How old are you?"

"Eighteen."

There was a clatter of mess-tins on the landing. I said: "That's our soup-ration coming up."

"Is the food good here?"

"You can judge for yourself in a moment."

I got up and stood ready, not only to collect my soup, but to make sure I shut the door myself.

The German soldier only gave me one ration. I pointed at Gimenez sitting on his bucket, and got a second lot without any trouble. Then I gently shut the door, and heard the guard lock it a moment later.

"Here's your meal, Gimenez." I offered him the mess-tin (it was only half-full) and a slice of bread with a scrape of margarine smeared over it.

He stared at the mess-tin and the black bread and said: "Is that all?"

"That's all. You'll get the same tomorrow, too. The soup looks a bit thicker than usual. Go on, try it. You must be famished."

In a few seconds the mess-tin was scraped bare and the bread gone, every last crumb of it.

I was suffering from very mixed emotions. I was delighted to have the company of another human being, yet agonised at the thought that my project would have to be postponed. I still had not wholly steeled myself, in any case, to carry it out; yet the memory of the morning's events made action imperative. Instinctively I played for time; I wanted leisure to resolve this mental and emotional turmoil.

"Take this, you're still hungry," I said, and broke a piece of my bread off. He took it, gratefully.

"We'll put the mess-tins and spoons here by the door. They go out into the corridor tomorrow, when morning coffee's brought round. It isn't anything like coffee really—just black water, but it's not bad. Where are you from, by the way?"

"My family own a farm near Dijon."

I said: "What military service have you done?"

"I'm in the L.V.F."

I stared at him. The L.V.F. was a so-called volunteer body raised by the Germans.

He went on: "I joined some time ago. I couldn't be sent to the Russian front; I failed my medical exam. But I went through the training course at Versailles."

"You were medically unfit, you mean?"

"Not completely. The Germans used me for light duties. For example, on some trains they have carriages reserved for German troops. My job was to stop French passengers using them."

I asked him if his parents were still alive.

"Yes—both of them; and I've got one small sister."

"Do they know what you've been doing?"

"No."

As we talked, I was studying his face in minute detail, trying to assess his character from his changes of expression and the way he reacted to my remarks.

"It's bedtime now," I said. "We'd better make you comfortable. Take off your tunic and roll it up as a pillow. That's right. Those are German Army boots you're wearing, aren't they? Good leather, iron-tipped heels, fine workmanship. Better than those my men had."

"You were a soldier too, then?"

"I was an officer."

Gimenez lay down on the floor of the cell. Gingerly, I lowered myself on to the bed. Gradually all noise died away in the prison. The sentries had been posted outside; we could hear their footsteps echoing across the empty courtyard.

Gimenez asked me what the noise was.

"Only the German sentries. Go to sleep now. No more talking."

His breathing gradually became louder and more regular; he was asleep. In the half-light his body was silhouetted grotesquely against the opposite wall, a vague, hunched shape swathed in a blanket.

Was he a friend or an enemy?

Conditions in the prison had obviously surprised him. His startled and bewildered expression, the nervousness he betrayed, all suggested that this was the first time he had found himself in such surroundings, or been in close contact with a convict. He was young enough to excite my sympathy, but there was a physical maturity about him which showed in his face and made me think twice about the way I should treat him. He was neither a boy nor a man, it seemed—and certainly not an ordinary prisoner. To put a member of the L.V.F. in my cell the day I was sentenced to death was surely something more than a coincidence. I had been in solitary confinement for five months; and they chose this of all days to give me a companion.

Was Timann hoping to get more detailed information out of me by this crudely stupid device? It was not impossible. If Gimenez was in fact a stool-pigeon, he would call the guard as soon as he discovered my plan to escape. Against all my expectations I had been brought back to the cell where all my equipment was hidden. Now what was I to do?

Fate obviously intended this as a warning. I could not wait till the Germans came to carry me off to face a firing-squad. I must act at once. The whole floor knew about my plans. I might be removed at any moment. The moon was on the wane, and my last rope could be constructed in a few hours. Everything was ready; to delay any longer would merely lengthen the odds against me. Time might pass more quickly in Gimenez's company, but what did that matter? The thing was to escape: with him or without him, but in any case as soon as possible. I must not give up now.

Tomorrow, I thought, I'll try and find out what sort of chap Gimenez really is. The day after that I'll tell him my plan. And the third day—out. Three days is the absolute limit.

Having come to this decision, I fell into a troubled sleep.

"Did you have a good night, Gimenez?" I said. It was early morning, and the guard was blowing sharp blasts on his whistle in the corridor.

"It was pretty hard lying, and the concrete was cold."

"The cell's got to be tidied up and swept now. I'll do it."

I followed my usual daily routine. The blankets I folded neatly and stacked on the mattress. But now, prominently displayed on top of them, was Gimenez's German tunic. Then I took the little broom and swept the floor carefully, depositing the dust in the bucket. I took particular care to hang my towel up above the door.

"Coffee'll be coming presently. It's going to be a fine day, don't you think? Look how blue the sky is. One more fine day in this place—"

He said: "Do we get anything to eat with the coffee?"

"No. But we get half a mess-tin of soup at mid-day. Nothing till then. Let's have a flea-hunt. Did they keep you awake?"

"No, but I felt them crawling over my skin. They've bitten me, too. Look."

"That's nothing. You ought to have seen de Pury the day after he got here. He was as red as a boiled lobster. He's in 119. You'll see him presently when we go out. He's completely bald."

"What is he?"

"A Protestant minister. We've got a Catholic priest, too; they're both in the same cell. Are you a believer?"

"I learnt my catechism. And my mother goes to Mass every Sunday."

I sighed. "It must be fine weather in your part of the country too. What'll your family be doing on the farm now? The harvest's over. Picking the grapes, I suppose?"

"We've only got a small vineyard. We mostly breed cattle."

"I come from Haute-Savoie. We haven't got any vineyards up there, it's too high in the mountains. But when I was a small boy I used to go down sometimes and pick grapes in the valley. I love grapes, don't you? It'd be fun to go grape-harvesting together, wouldn't it?"

He said: "I'm fond of grapes myself. I remember at home—"

"Careful, here comes the coffee. They might beat us up if they caught us talking."

When the door opened I put out our empty mess-tins and collected two full ones. I closed the door gently. Gimenez was sitting on the bucket, his chin resting on one hand, still dreaming (I presume) about his family vineyard.

"Here you are," I said. "It's *ersatz*—made from barley or corn-husks, I think. It's got no taste, but it is hot. Up in my part of the country we can still get real coffee. It's not far from the Swiss border, and things can still be smuggled across."

"There's no sugar in it. It's ages since I had a cup of good milky coffee with sugar in it."

"Didn't the Germans give you milk in your coffee?" I asked.

"What a hope!"

"But the food was all right?"

"Not too bad. But we were always ravenous. All that marching and drill—"

"Why didn't you tell your family you were at Versailles?"

"My father would have thrashed me to death if he'd known I was working for the Germans. I ran away from home. I didn't know what I wanted to do. I never thought I'd end up in the L.V.F. Our house is quite near the station. My mother came after me. She tried to make me go back home. But I managed to shake her off, and catch the train."

I asked him how long it was since he had written to his mother. Four months, he said.

"Send her a letter as soon as you can. Just say where you are. She must be worried to death wondering what's happened to you."

He said: "I ran away once before, last year, with a friend of mine. We wanted to get over the border into Spain and then make our way to England. We were caught near Bayonne. There was a big river we couldn't cross because it was flooded. The police took us to Bordeaux, and we were each sentenced to a month in gaol."

"Did you serve the full sentence?"

"No. They let us out after a fortnight."

"What did you do then?"

"I went back home. My friend made for Marseilles."

"Why Marseilles? Did he live there?"

"No. He thought he might find some way of getting across to North Africa."

"Look out, here comes the guard. We're going out for exercise now. You take the bucket. Just do what everyone else does. Don't forget to ask for a mattress. And have a wash!"

I stood in front of him, close to the door, so that I could open it myself when it was unlocked.

"I see you have company," Jeantet whispered to me when we were waiting in the corridor.

"Yes. A young fellow."

"How are you going to manage with him there?"

"I haven't thought yet."

Then we trooped down into the courtyard. Ten minutes later we were back again.

On the staircase I noticed Gimenez making signs to another prisoner, a young man of about twenty I had never seen before. Apparently he was in our wing too.

When we were back in our cell I reminded him about the mattress. As the duty sergeant passed by to lock the doors, Gimenez indicated to him that he had nowhere to sleep. He pointed at my mattress, and managed to convey the idea that he wanted one as well.

The sergeant escorted him down the corridor. A short while later he returned, with a mattress slung over one shoulder. He had a blanket, too.

"There," he said, and dumped them on the floor.

"We'd better stack them on top of each other during the day. It'll leave us more room in the cell."

The cover, I noticed, was made not of linen, but coarse raffia. This did not matter. The important thing was that, by putting this second mattress on the bed, I could leave the cell looking quite normal on the day I made my second rope. The loss of my cover would not be noticed. I could also use this new mattress to hide the other rope and the grappling-irons—not to mention the straw and dust from my own mattress.

I said: "You can have a comfortable nap now. Did you manage to wash?"

"I rinsed my face in cold water, but I've got nothing to dry myself with, not even a handkerchief."

"I'll give you half my towel tomorrow morning. I wash with the same one every day. That one hanging on the door's a spare. I never use it."

"Is this the only exercise we get?"

"That's right. About ten minutes."

"At Bordeaux we were always out in the courtyard or working in the prison shop. The food was better there, too."

I said: "I was just thinking of the baker's shop in our village. You can smell the new bread a mile off—gorgeous stuff, straight out of the oven, piping hot. It's a fertile district; we never go short of anything."

"My part of the country's the same. If I was at home I'd get good milky coffee, white bread, butter, everything."

"Why do we sit here starving when we could get all we want outside? Savoy isn't so far from Lyons—about a hundred miles, no more. Three and a half hours by train. Dijon's quite close, too—the next station after Mâcon and Chalon."

Gimenez said: "You've forgotten to mark up your calendar to-day."

"So I have. Wait a moment."

I extracted my pencil from its hiding-place.

"That's a good place to keep it. Is there a chimney there, or what?"

"A ventilation shaft. The bucket used to be kept in there, and the air-hole was meant to stop it stinking too badly. Our bucket's too big to go in." I paused and added: "Pencils are forbidden in here. The Germans paraded us outside one day and told us anyone who was caught with a pencil would be shot. I had one, but I kept it."

"All that fuss about a pencil?"

"One of us had smuggled a letter out in some dirty laundry. They were furious."

"You've hidden yours well," he said. "They'll never find it."

"You can use it, too. If I'm transferred I'll bequeath it to you. Can you see where it is? Here, you can feel the place."

I guided his hand towards a tiny hole inside the air-vent. This test had proved successful; he had raised no objections. He was already my accomplice in crime. I spent the morning questioning him about what was going on outside, especially at the front; but it was impossible to get any useful information out of him. He was completely ignorant of public events. He did not even know whether the Allies had landed or not.

I said: "I've been shut up here for four months, so I don't know how the war's going; but I'm convinced the Germans will lose it. They've got everyone against them now: the Russians, the English, the Americans, everyone. They'll be crushed by sheer weight of numbers."

"Perhaps. But the Germans are good fighters."

"No better than anyone else. I'll give you an example. In December 1939 I was commanding a detachment of scouts. The Germans attacked us with a whole company. They outnumbered us by ten to one, yet they turned tail and ran like rabbits. They'll run again before they're through. I got the Legion of Honour as a result of that little affair. Look; you can see the red ribbon still on my lapel. That's what the Germans have really got against me. I was a good soldier. You could do as well yourself. You're young and strong, you want to get out of this place—"

He said: "I think I would make a good soldier. The sergeant-major at Versailles always told me so."

"It's a pity you made such a bad choice."

"What do you mean?"

"I mean the uniform you chose to wear. It won't get you a lighter sentence, you know."

"What have I got to be afraid of at my age?"

"Your youth means nothing here. You're just another prisoner. How long are you in for?"

"I don't know. Not long, I suppose."

I said: "When the Germans put someone in prison it's never a short business. I've seen women and old men who'd been here for months. What could they have done? To the Germans you are, quite simply, a Frenchman. The uniform you wear and the work you've done for them means nothing. You'll be here for a long time, possibly for years."

"Are you serious?"

"Take my case. I've done nothing. But I've been here for five months. Every time they interrogated me I protested that I was innocent. It made no difference at all. Ah. Here comes our soup."

The duty sergeant opened the door, and I got our two mess-tins shortly afterwards from one of the fatigue-party. Then the door was locked once more.

"Is that all we get?"

"I'm afraid so. Are you hungry?"

"I could eat five—no, ten of those rations."

"I'll wangle a double ration tonight. It's easy. You'll see."

"They starve you in this place," he said plaintively.

"Do you remember the fresh bread I was telling you about this morning, and all the good food we could get outside?"

"But we'd have to be free—"

"Of course. I tried to escape once. They beat me up when they caught me." I told him the story in a few words.

"You didn't stand a chance."

"Maybe not. But if you were in a Gestapo car and got the chance to jump out, what would *you* do?"

"Jump."

"Even if there was a guard on your heels, taking pot-shots at you with a revolver?"

He said: "Yes. I think so."

"You're a good boy. I'm glad they put you in my cell. You've got guts. That's very useful."

I was getting a stronger hold over Gimenez the whole time. Things were going very well. He was desperately hungry: I played on this weakness constantly with talk about good food. He was fond of his mother, so I constantly brought up the subject of his family. I tempted him with the prospect of everything we could get outside that was unobtainable in prison. I drew the blackest possible picture of our present situation, and rhapsodised over the pleasures which freedom would bring.

"The fleas must have had a field-day on you last night. You've been scratching all morning." I examined him more closely. "What are those black specks on your leg?"

"I don't know."

A careful inspection revealed that he was crawling with lice.

"Lice, my God! You're disgusting. Can't you wash properly? You run away from your family, you work for the bloody Germans, and to crown it all you bring a load of stinking lice in with you. Haven't we got enough to put up with without that? Your body's as filthy as your rotten little mind."

"Lice!" he repeated, horrified.

"Yes, lice. Body-lice. They burrow into the skin, especially where there's any hair, and breed like wildfire. Pull one off and put it on this piece of paper."

"It's not so easy." He scratched away for a moment, and then deposited a louse on the paper I held ready.

"Look at it," I said. "These filthy black vermin act as carriers for every kind of disease. The big ones are black, the small ones are exactly the same colour as your skin, and you can never spot them. The M.O. of my regiment was very hot on lice. Strip off and put your clothes over there in the corner. You must be crawling with them."

"Will they get into my clothes?"

"They get everywhere. Generally the only way to get rid of them is to burn the clothes they've infected."

When he had taken off his clothes I could not help feeling sorry for him; he was fairly swarming with the creatures. I realised at once that I could not help catching them off him. What was to be done? I could hardly tell the guards; they would at once disinfect the cell, and that would mean the removal of the mattress which held all my precious equipment. No, I had to use this incident as a fresh inducement to him to escape with me.

"To delouse yourself you need to shave all your body-hair off, take several hot baths, and burn all your clothes. But it's an impossible job here. There must be lice in every cell; you'd have to burn down the prison."

"Then you think I picked them up in here?"

"Certainly not. Up till now I haven't seen one myself. You've only been really crawling since yesterday. You must have caught them in some dirty hotel, or perhaps off a woman. If she passed even one on to you, it could breed hundreds more."

He said: "It must have been a woman. My friend and I used to visit a brothel regularly in Versailles. I remember I went to one in Lyons the evening before I was arrested."

"I thought all the brothels had been closed down."

"There are still some kept going for the Germans. Since we were in the L.V.F. we were allowed to use them."

"That was it, then, obviously. These places are always dirty. But now I come to think of it there's a very good one at Annemasse, close to the frontier. From what the local inhabitants tell me, the girls are all very pretty."

He asked me whether this brothel still existed.

"Yes—at any rate, one of my friends told me so, just before I was arrested. If we could get out of here, we could celebrate our liberation there."

"But that needs money." He was a practical boy, it seemed.

"Money's no object. There's plenty of it where I come from. If we were free we could live like kings and have a high old time generally."

This time Gimenez heard the soup coming before I did. He reminded me of the promise I had made earlier to get him a double portion. I said I would try. As soon as I got our ration, I passed the mess-tins quickly to Gimenez and stood hopefully in the doorway again. An orderly gave me two more without even looking at me.

"There. We're really being spoilt this evening."

"Well done. I'm ravenous. How on earth can you keep your end up on this kind of diet? The whole set-up's impossible—starvation, fleas, lice, no fresh air, not even proper washing facilities. I'm lucky to have you around. It'd have been fun serving under you."

"You may get the chance yet," I said. "Stick close to me and you won't go far wrong. I can promise you an interesting life and plenty of action. Look at my hand. No—this one, my left hand. Do you see that line? It's the fate line. Straight, sharp-cut, a lovely fate line. Nothing can happen to me, I'm accident-proof. What's more, I bring other people good luck. Now show me yours."

He extended it, palm uppermost.

"Wonderful! A most successful hand. We're both lucky by nature. We could do great things together. You saw how it was with the soup. We've got two rations each, and everyone else has to make do with one. In all the other cells they're miserable as hell. They've resigned themselves to prison life. We've got better things to think about. Women. Freedom."

"Freedom?"

"Freedom," I repeated, with great emphasis. "Didn't you tell me this morning that you'd escape if you got the chance?"

"Out of a moving car, perhaps—if you were with me."

"It would be easier with two of us."

He said, doubtfully: "Always supposing we were transferred at the same time . . ."

"There are other ways. Look: I've been thinking out how to escape ever since the Gestapo first clapped the handcuffs on me. I think about it night and day. When you've been born and bred in the country, like us, and always breathed good fresh air and worked hard with your hands, you can't bear to be cooped up. I'm not the sort of person to sit around waiting for things to happen, and I don't think you are, either. And don't kid yourself that the Germans feel any sympathy for the miserable kind of bastard who just vegetates. On the contrary, it's our sort they respect. They beat me up when I tried to escape: that was the routine. But the Gestapo agent who interrogated me told me afterwards that he admired my spirit."

I had to play down the risks for him. He must not think for one moment that if we failed it would inevitably mean a firing-squad.

Darkness was beginning to fall. Jeantet had not called me up for our usual evening chat; he was clearly suspicious of the new arrival. Tomorrow, when we went out, I would reassure him.

"Let's go to sleep now," I said to Gimenez.

He grunted. "This double mattress is very comfortable," he murmured. "I shall dream of a seven-course dinner and a wonderful girl . . ."

"I've got more than that to dream about," I said.

My programme was going according to plan. I fell asleep, pleased with my day's work. In his corner Gimenez snored tranquilly. It was August 23.

I woke very early: the first morning light was only just beginning to filter into our cell.

To sleep on an idea often induces second thoughts about it. I was beginning to feel uneasy; my fine optimism was evaporating. In a few hours, Gimenez would know everything. Was it possible that he might give me away? The idea put me into a sweat of apprehension. To be so near my object and then fail through a simple error of judgment!

No. It was impossible. I couldn't be wrong now. I had to go on, with or without Gimenez's help. I had to escape. Even if he wanted to give me away, he could only do it during a meal or at morning exercise. It was up to me to make sure he never got near a German guard. I would handle the rations, not him. When we went out I would stick close to him. If at the last moment I felt he was lukewarm about the whole thing, I would leave him there asleep and go without him.

I looked at his face, clear now in the morning light. At the same time I felt the hard outline of the biggest grappling-iron under my mattress-cover. I put my hand over it.

"Gimenez," I called. "Gimenez, wake up!" I wanted to talk to him, and silence the unpleasant doubts which had been troubling me. "Time to get up!"

"Already?" he said, stretching. "Nothing's stirring."

"It's broad daylight. Did you sleep well?"

"I dreamed I was a free man."

"Sometimes," I said, "dreams and reality come very close to each other. Let's tidy up the cell."

Whistles blew; coffee appeared; I put our four mess-tins out in the corridor. When we went out I whispered to Jeantet: "Come up to the fanlight this evening. I think everything's going to be all right."

"Knock on the wall first."

I had a few quick words with Grimaud in the wash-house. I told him that I was ready, and that my plan would come off at any moment now.

"Whatever happens, I must get away," I said.

He wished me good luck.

"No, don't say that!"

The stage was all set for the play to begin. I had to make a huge effort to master my nervous apprehension and behave normally. I must not betray my inner tension by a single action or change of expression. I trailed up the stairs in the usual way, my brimming jam-jar in one hand, my towel in the other (at least, what was left of it), clutching a small sliver of soap.

"Hardly five minutes today," Gimenez grumbled as he put down the bucket.

"No, they don't let us out for long. We've got another day here yet. One more day: I'll mark it on the calendar. If you want to pass the time, try killing some of those lice you've got."

He squatted down on the floor and set about this loathsome task. I decided the moment was ripe to launch my attack.

"You told me yesterday that if you had the chance to escape you'd take it, didn't you?"

"That's right. I wouldn't miss an opportunity like that. Why do you ask? Do you think we're going to be moved? Will there be another car to jump out of?"

"No, we're not going to be moved."

"Well, what do you mean, then?"

"There's another way we can get out of Montluc."

"I don't understand. Unless we grow wings it's impossible."

"Gimenez," I said, "it is possible. I'm going to show you how. Look."

There was no one in the corridor. I took down the towel from the door, and then, without moving anything, showed him the work which had cost me such efforts two months before.

Then I knocked out the wedges with my spoon-handle, and removed my "shutter," thus exposing the upper tenon of the central panel.

I sketched a rough plan of the prison on the wall and described our route in detail. Next, I unpacked all my equipment, and showed him how I had solved each problem in turn. His eyes grew wider and wider; gingerly he examined in turn the rope, the grappling-irons, and everything else, complimenting me repeatedly on my patience and ingenuity.

"You see, Gimenez, you can do something with nothing if you put your mind to it."

"It's wonderful!"

I said: "I have absolute confidence—in myself, in my plan, in every piece of equipment I've made. We've got all the trump cards. We're bound to pull it off. You're in it with me now. You can't say no. I'm determined to go through with it, and you're going with me."

"I have a free choice," he said.

"You have no choice at all," I said, and clapped a friendly hand on his back.

"When do you aim to go?"

"Tomorrow night."

Several times during this critical exchange I thought I heard an unusual noise going on somewhere in the prison—a distant, muffled knocking, some workman in the courtyard perhaps, or in a ground-floor cell. I took no more notice of it, and about midday the noise stopped.

But in the afternoon it began again, and seemed to be coming closer. Now I was really alarmed. The knocking became louder and sharper; and I suddenly realised that they were testing the doors. I lay with one ear to the ground and heard a cell-door opened on the floor below, several metallic bangs, the closing of the door, a short pause, and then the same noise again.

"What is it?" Gimenez asked.

"Nothing," I said. "They must be checking the grilles."

He did not pursue the point. He was obviously unaware of the grave danger threatening us. I hastily set about checking every detail of my camouflage.

"That's sensible," said Gimenez. "Supposing they decided to test the door, too, while they were in here . . ." He stretched himself out on the bed.

The hours which followed were an isolated nightmare the effect of which it is almost impossible to describe. I wanted to put my head in my hands and cry; the next moment misery would change to frustrated rage. Such violent emotions breed madness: I felt my control slowly slipping away. I sat in front of the door, eyes staring, while the last moments of my life, as I thought, were hammered away. I simply could not believe such a disaster was possible.

All my patient toil, the risks I had run, my whole meticulously worked out plan, the agonies I had suffered—were they all in vain? It was impossible, it couldn't be true.

I was very near weeping. Heavy drops of sweat rolled down my face. They had reached our wing now. I leant forward with all my strength against the weak central panel.

I thought about de Pury, Grimaud, Jeantet and Duflot. The footsteps were very close now. Four cells away. Three. Two. Mine now. This was it. There were voices outside. Someone tapped the wood of the door perfunctorily with his fingers. I held my breath. The steps moved on. They did not stop outside 109 either. I heard them cross to the cells on the other side of the corridor, and realised that we were safe.

I peered through the spyhole, and saw two men staring at one of the doors: an unknown civilian, and a soldier who carried a hammer and a bunch of keys. The soldier opened the door. Then the civilian took the hammer, went inside, and tapped each of the bolt-heads in turn. This done, the door was locked once more, and the workman tightened the screws outside. Then they went on to the next cell. I came away from the spyhole, wiping my sweating face.

Gimenez was asleep on the bed, unaware of the drama which had just taken place.

Tomorrow had to be the day. It was sheer madness to wait any longer. If the rope I needed to cross the perimeter had been ready, I would have gone that same night.

After supper I talked to Jeantet through the fanlight.

"I was scared about your door this afternoon," he said.

"It was a miracle. But miracles don't happen twice. I'm going to break out tomorrow night."

"I think you're wise. But what about your young friend?"

"He's made up his mind to come with me. If I have reason to doubt his loyalty at the last moment—well, I shall have to do something extremely unpleasant. I only hope God will forgive me. But I've reached the limit of my endurance, Eugene. And Fate's given me a very clear warning not to delay."

He said: "I was scared stiff, you know. I haven't got over it yet."

He paused, then went on in a different voice: "When you go, you'll be taking all my joys and hopes and fears with you. You'll leave an irreplaceable gap in my life. But if you didn't go, it would be still worse, in a way. One thing I've learnt is that to make any sacrifice worth while you must give up everything. You told me yourself that the struggle must go on to the end.

"So retreat is a kind of betrayal. You've got to go if you're going to remain true to yourself, and justify all the ideas you taught me to believe. We've all given up in this place. You'll give us new hope. I can't bear the thought of losing you, but you must go. One of us at least can show our enemies that we're not beaten into submission yet."

"Thank you, Eugene. You're a good friend. I'm going to have a shot at it tomorrow. If I succeed, you'll be able to tell it from the way the Germans behave. I'll let them know outside how you've helped me. If I fail, you can bear witness that at least I fought well."

He said: "You're going to bring it off. I'm certain of that."

I ignored this. "You must go and visit my family," I said. "You must see my wife and children and tell them everything you know."

"There won't be any need to. You'll get out all right."

"Supposing I do, Eugene—is there anything I could do for you, anyone I could—"

"No. There's nobody. You're the only friend I've got."

"I'll say good-bye to you before I go," I said.

"Till tomorrow, then."

As I climbed down I heard Jeantet shifting his bed back into place next door. Heavy-hearted, I sat down and buried my face in my hands.

"What's the matter?" Gimenez asked. "You're even paler than usual. You look as if you were about to burst into tears."

"Oh, nothing. I'm just a bit depressed at the thought of leaving Jeantet. We've been together a long time now."

"Why don't you stay?"

"No!" I said vehemently. "Look, here's our programme for tomorrow. We'll get up very early, before reveille, and work on my mattress. We'll have to cut it into strips and empty all the stuffing into yours. Then we'll sweep the cell. We'll make the rope during the morning and immediately after lunch. Then we'll shave and cut our hair. When we've had supper we'll test the rope, get the equipment ready—and go."

"Shouldn't we leave a note saying we've gone?"

A humorist too, it seemed.

"We'll send them a postcard. Don't forget that we must look like ordinary civilians when we're out in the streets. We'll have to take our coats and shoes with us."

He reminded me that he had a German tunic.

"That doesn't matter. It might even come in useful. Bring your forage-cap too. We'll make three parcels—one for the long rope, one for the coats, and one for our shoes. You'll be responsible for the coats and shoes. I'll take everything else."

"How do we get out on to the roof?"

"I've got all that worked out. I'll be first out of the cell. You'll pass me the parcels through the door, and I'll hide them in the latrines opposite. I'll tie one end of the light rope—that's the one we're going to make tomorrow—round my waist. Then I'll climb out on to the roof. You'll tie the parcels on to the other end of the rope, and I'll haul them up. Then I'll let the rope down again for you. Loop it under your shoulders and I'll help you up, like a rock-climber. Got the idea?"

He nodded. I said: "We mustn't forget the spare grappling-iron."

"Couldn't we put it in with the long rope? Then we'd have all our escape equipment in one bundle and our personal effects in the other."

"Good idea. Tell you something else. When you go out for exercise tomorrow, take the jam-jar as well as the bucket, and bring it back full of water."

"What about you?"

"I'll take a mess-tin and fill that too. We'll need drinking-water, and we've got to wash and shave. Now let's go to sleep. Our last night here, Gimenez. Think of it. Tomorrow we'll sleep between clean white sheets."

"After a really good meal," he said dreamily.

"And plenty to drink."

"Good night, André."

"Good night. I'm going out into the corridor later. If you wake up don't be alarmed."

"Where are you going?"

"Not far."

I got little sleep. Had I prepared my plan in sufficiently minute detail? Had I forgotten anything? It would be useful, as Jeantet had suggested, to muffle the grappling-irons with some cloth padding to stop them scraping loudly on the edges of the roof and the walls. I also decided to add a weight to the one that would have to be thrown across the perimeter. This would ensure that the hook caught in the guttering at the first attempt.

There was a lot I still had to teach Gimenez—how to crawl Indian fashion, walk noiselessly on shingle, swarm down the rope, and cross the perimeter using a monkey-hold. An operation of this kind could only succeed if rehearsed and planned down to the smallest detail. We had to be able to place absolute trust in our equipment.

It had been dark for some time now. I got up to pay a visit to cell 119, where de Pury lived.

Quickly I dismantled the door, putting its component parts down neatly in the order of their removal. Then, in the usual way, I arranged a blanket over the gap to stop the moonlight shining through into the corridor. I crawled out on hands and knees into the gallery, after listening long and carefully for any suspicious sounds inside the building.

I called softly to de Pury through his spy-hole. A faint grunt answered me. I called again.

"Coming, coming." I heard de Pury yawn enormously. Then he padded quietly to the spy-hole.

"This is the last time I shall visit you," I said. "I'm going to make a break for it tomorrow night."

"With your new companion?"

"Yes. Look, I'm going to slide a piece of paper under the door. It's my will. Would you—"

"Of course," he said. "I promise. If you succeed, go and see a colleague of mine named Durand. The address is 30, Montée de la Boucle."

I repeated this carefully.

"I shall pray for you," de Pury said.

"Thank you. Good-bye."

We whispered each word softly and slowly, spacing out the syllables. After speaking myself, I put my ear against the spy-hole so as not to miss anything. Then I slid the sheet of paper under the door and went back to the other end of the corridor, close to the landing. Here I listened cautiously for a moment before finally returning to my cell.

"You were away a long time," Gimenez said.

"I've been for a stroll round," I said. Then I reassembled the door, not hurrying over the job, and lay down again.

The dawn had hardly broken when I woke again. The prison was still asleep. The only sound was the occasional footfall of a sentry outside. I shook Gimenez, and whispered in his ear: "Gimenez, Gimenez, wake up!"

He stretched himself, and mumbled something about it still being dark.

"Wake up! We've got to start our preparations."

"Preparations for what?" he asked. He was still half-asleep.

"For leaving tonight."

"Tonight?"

"Get up, man. We've got to empty the stuffing out of my mattress into yours, cut the cover into strips and clean up the cell. And it's all got to be done before breakfast."

"I remember now," he said, rubbing his eyes.

"Come on, hurry up!"

"It's a wonderful piece of work you've done there. It's very tempting . . ."

I had to impose my will on him. It was mere chance that had

made him my companion in adventure; I would not have taken him by choice. Now, after his earlier enthusiasm, he seemed to be backing out. I explained the position to him in a cold, cutting voice, letting him feel my anger and the concealed threat behind my words.

"You're coming with me whether it's 'tempting' or not. You have no choice in the matter."

"I'm free to make up my own mind."

"Oh no, you're not. We did all this work together, you know."

"What do you mean?"

"You are my accomplice, Gimenez. I strongly advise you not to think of denouncing me. If you do, you can rest assured that I shall invent a convincing enough story to get you shot too."

"What do you take me for?" he said, angry himself now.

"We're going to get away with this. I wouldn't take such risks if I wasn't sure of it. But if we were caught through your stupidity, I should say that you'd helped me—that in fact, I couldn't have completed the equipment without you."

He said: "Let's get to work. You're in command here."

"Quick, then. It's nearly light."

Gimenez, now thoroughly tamed, set about the job with positive enthusiasm. I cut the seam of the mattress with a razor-blade, but carefully did not pull the material apart: tearing linen makes quite a loud noise. Gimenz meanwhile pulled out the straw and dust in fistfulls, and shoved it into his raffia coverlet, which gradually began to swell out. The mattress disintegrated rapidly; soon all that was left of it was a piece of cloth four yards by one. I shook it out, brushed away the bits of straw still stuck to it, and got Gimenez to help me fold it. Time was passing all too quickly.

"Now we'd better hide all this."

The cloth and rope and string we put on the bedstead, and then covered them over with the second mattress. On top of this I carefully laid a blanket. Then I swept out the cell. It looked exactly as it did every day.

"That went off well," I said. "Did you see how strong that cloth is?"

"There's a lot of it, too."

"Only just enough, in fact. We'll cut it into three strips. Each strip'll make us about three yards of rope. That means two joins, not counting the grappling-iron at the end. It'll take no time at all to make, and you could hang a ton weight on it without its breaking."

Gimenez said: "I'm sorry about just now. I wasn't properly awake."

"I must say I was a bit surprised. You were all for it last night. Look, you simply must obey me, blindly. Whether we succeed or fail depends entirely on your attitude. Look at me."

He raised his eyes to mine.

I said, firmly: "Tomorrow at this time we shall be free men."

After coffee we had an hour before morning exercise.

"Get out the cloth and we'll cut it up."

We unfolded it and cut it into strips of equal width with a razor-blade, following the pencil marks I had made earlier. Then each piece was separately folded and returned to its hiding-place.

I noticed a few threads and specks of dust on the floor, and made Gimenez sweep them up.

Morning exercise went off in the normal way, but de Pury, Grimaud and Jeantet never took their eyes off me. Jeantet in particular had a heart-rendingly desolate expression on his face. When we returned he stopped for a moment outside his door, and I outside mine. We looked at each other, but said nothing. There was no need to.

Then, just before he went in, he said in a tremulous voice, eyes downcast: "Come up to the fanlight once more before you go."

Gimenez had, as I told him to, brought back my jam-jar brimming with water. I had watched him out of the corner of my eye all through the exercise period, and taken care to let him know I was near him. It would have been only too easy for him to point a finger at me and say: "That man is planning to escape!"

There was nothing strained about his behaviour, rather the opposite: he was so natural that he gave me confidence.

We got to work at once.

"Gimenez, you sit there on the bed, in that corner, and hold the end of the strip firm while I twist it. If there's anyone coming, push the whole thing into the earth-closet. We can't be seen in this part of the cell, anyway."

We unfolded the first strip, got out my two balls of string, and began to make our rope. As with the previous one, I folded the cloth into four thicknesses, turning the edges in towards the middle. I tied it firmly at Gimenez's end, then twisted it into a strong, thin rope, which I bound round with a double thickness of string to maintain torsion. Every three or four inches, to stop it coming apart and reinforce it still further, I bound it tightly with wire. This primitive method of rope-making proved both fast and efficient. As each length was completed we pulled on it as hard as we could and found it stood up wonderfully to our combined strength. Occasionally we paused to listen, then returned to our labours.

"It'll soon be finished," I said from time to time. Gimenez, now engrossed in the whole thing, was obviously doing his best to help.

In fact, the long strips of cloth and the string I had prepared beforehand considerably lessened our trouble. In endless rotation I folded, twisted, tied knots, cut loose ends and then folded again; but all the time a fine, light, supple rope was slowly lengthening under my tired hands.

In two or three hours we had used up all the cloth from my mattress-cover.

"We'd better measure it," Gimenez said.

To my great surprise it was only twenty-three feet long.

"It isn't enough. We need about seven foot more to make it the right size. You've got a pullover. Give me your shirt and that other one in the box. We've still got two towels if we run out of material."

"Why not use the blanket?"

"The rope would be too thick for this job. It'd be weighty enough to carry, let alone sling across from wall to wall."

His khaki shirt and the two towels were cut up and added to the rest. The total length now topped thirty feet. It was more than enough.

Our midday meal passed off without incident. Immediately afterwards, while the guards were at lunch, we tested the rope. Despite our most violent efforts we failed to break it. Once again I examined every inch with great care and reinforced any section that seemed in the least doubtful. Then I attached one end to a grappling-iron —the heavy one that would go across the perimeter. I strengthened the part of the rope that went through the loop with a piece of thick material cut from one of Gimenez's puttees. I made the knot as strong as possible, but left the grappling-iron with a certain amount of play. This would make it easier to hook it on to the wall. To this end also I weighted it with a cobble I had picked up in the courtyard. When the grappling-iron was lobbed over the wall and the rope gently pulled, the hook would automatically lie point downmost. To muffle any noise it might make I lagged it with the rest of Gimenez's puttee. We treated the other two grappling-irons in a similar way, and disposed of them in the earth-closet or under the bed.

Judging by Gimenez's enthusiasm, and the questions he asked me, I reckoned that he would in fact follow me when the time came. He seemed as impatient as I was, and took an equal pride in the completion of our equipment.

"My God, it's strong," he said admiringly. "Who would guess you could make things like this in a prison cell?"

"That is the prisoner's peculiar art: making something out of nothing. Can you imagine Fränzel's face when he sees those ropes hanging there tomorrow morning?"

"I certainly can," said Gimenez. "I don't think we'd better let him catch us again."

"No."

I shivered; the words seemed unlucky.

During the afternoon we shaved. As far as I was concerned this was a most unpleasant operation. The blade squeaked and bent in its wooden holder. But after much perseverance my skin began to appear again. It was extraordinarily white, with red dabs here and there where the razor had nicked me. Gimenez, who was holding the little piece of mirror for me, seemed amused.

"It's all very well for you to laugh. You haven't got a beard—just bum-fluff."

"Rubbish. Here, feel. I'm a grown man."

I said: "We'll know more about that tomorrow."

While he sat on the bucket I cut his hair. It was a difficult operation. I smoothed down his matted locks as well as I could, and scraped away at them with the razor. Then, to please him, I trimmed the sparse soft growth on his cheeks and chin. This done we changed places, and he did his best with me.

"Hold the blade nearly flat and follow the natural line of the hair," I told him. "That'll take off the worst of it and leave it looking fairly tidy."

He told me I had some white hairs.

"Those are only the first ones," I said.

To fill in time when we had finished I went over the whole plan with him once more, in every detail.

"Are you sure you know what you've got to do?"

"Of course. You've told me twice now."

"It doesn't necessarily follow. Remember, not the least noise. Just stick behind me and do what I do. If it takes two hours to cross the roof, that can't be helped. We mustn't give ourselves away. I forgot to tell you that it's covered with tarred gravel. You'll have to put your feet down in two separate movements, heel first, then the sole. Understand?"

He nodded.

"Right. Now I'll show you the Indian crawl. You have to feel your way with your hands, and wriggle your body forward smoothly. You mustn't use your feet. Like this."

I got down on the floor and demonstrated the movement. He watched for a moment, then tried it himself. He did it quite well.

"Breathe through your mouth. It makes less noise, and calms you down. Never forget that our worst enemy is silence, Gimenez. Nothing else matters much. Silence is the great invisible hazard. It's everywhere, lying in wait for us, ready to betray us if we make the least mistake. It'll get on your nerves horribly. On the other hand, the trains'll help us. They pass by every quarter of an hour, whistling like mad and making a tremendous noise. When you hear one coming, get ready to move."

About seven o'clock supper was served. I took the soup and bread, shut the door, and shared them out with Gimenez.

"Tomorrow the menu will improve considerably. That's a promise."

We ate slowly and in silence.

"It's not too bad tonight," Gimenez said at length, licking his lips.

As I swallowed every spoonful the thought that this might be my last meal in Montluc made it taste delicious.

"It's horrible stuff," I said.

We put the mess-tins away. While Gimenez was busy making a parcel of our coats and shoes, I signalled to Jeantet and went up to the fanlight.

"We're all set, Eugene," I said. "We made the last rope today. It's incredibly strong."

"Have you muffled the grappling-irons with cloth, as I told you?"

I said I had.

"Have you reinforced the section of the rope that'll have to take the strain on the parapet?"

I said I had.

"Have you briefed your companion thoroughly?"

"Of course."

"Have you—"

I interrupted him.

"Eugene—it breaks my heart to be leaving you here like this—"

He said: "Don't think about it. Don't let it weaken you. You've done enough for me already. You saved me from suicide and gave me something to live for. You showed me what character and courage and a sense of duty meant—"

"It was all there in you. You just never saw it."

"You're wrong. It's thanks to you that my life means something to me today. I could never ask more of you than that. Don't hesitate now. Don't look back. Go straight on. Tomorrow you'll be far away, and I shall miss you, God knows. But the thought of your achievement will be recompense enough for your loss."

I said: "I shall never forget our friendship, Eugene."

"I shall pray to God for your safety. Tell the world that there is nothing, nothing so precious as freedom. Good-bye, André, and good luck."

"Good-bye, Eugene."

"Knock on the wall just before you go."

"At the last stroke of ten. I promise."

I climbed down again, extremely moved by Jeantet's last words. Gimenez had finished the parcel. I checked it, and then we set about packing up the big rope. It had to be made into as small a parcel as possible so that it could go through the main skylight without difficulty; it also had to be done up in such a way that it could be unpacked in a matter of seconds. To solve this problem I tied the string in double bows; we could not afford to waste time over knots in the dark. I left one end out and fastened the spare hook to it, making sure that this, too, could be quickly removed when necessary.

Once I had reached the roof I intended to hang the roll containing the shorter rope on this hook, and let it down into the courtyard, thus leaving myself completely free and unhampered in my movements.

We ranged these parcels in a line along the wall, in the order in which Gimenez would pass them out to me: first the light rope, then the heavy one, and lastly our coats and shoes.

I gave Gimenez detailed instructions.

"When I pass you the boards and pieces of wood from the door, put them in that corner near the earth-closet, so that they don't get in our way."

"I understand," he said.

Slowly the hours chimed out in the stillness. All was quiet; the prison slept. The dismal, regular footfall of the sentries echoed on the cobbles.

Lights were lit in the town, and a dim glow penetrated into our cell.

Ten o'clock began to strike. I sprang to my feet, and nodded to Gimenez.

Seven; eight; nine; *ten*. Crouched in front of the door I counted the strokes. The infantryman ready to spring out of his trench, the parachutist slipping into space—both of them act instinctively, without thought; they lose their identity in a corporate movement, and are plunged at once into violent action. But I had no such support. My operation had to be carried out in cold blood. I was alone in this vast, menacing silence. My equipment was home-made, and I bore sole responsibility for my plan. The young man beside me symbolised the element of doubt and uncertainty. I had to remain absolutely cool-headed, controlling my enthusiasm, matching determination with patience. Every move had to be calculated logically, and executed at precisely the right moment. Only so could we ever cross the wall to freedom.

My heart was thudding violently against my rib-cage, and I felt myself trembling.

Gimenez was behind me, a little to my right. I tapped several times on the wall to tell Jeantet we were off, and heard a faint knocking in response.

As the last stroke faded I knocked out the wedges which held the boards in place. Now I was trembling no longer; the curtain had gone up, and the play was on.

11

Gimenez took the boards from me one after the other and stacked them away. In the half-light we could just see the faint, barred outline of the gallery rails; it was too dark to make out the cell doors on the other side. I put out my head and listened. Only the creaking of beds as sleepers turned over, and occasionally a bucket scraping along the floor, broke the silence—that hostile silence against which we had to struggle for what seemed like a century.

For two long minutes I remained motionless. Then I pushed one arm out into the corridor, turned on one side, and crawled forward like a snake. I stood up cautiously. The light was on down below; but, as usual, its feeble rays were swallowed up in the vast gloom of the hall.

Gimenez passed me the light rope, which I at once took over to the latrines. It was followed by the rest of our equipment. I went back to the cell door to help Gimenez. We both stood there for a moment, listening. All was still. Slowly we moved towards our starting-point.

I tied one end of the light rope round my waist—the end, that is, which had no grappling-iron attached to it. Three steps, and we were standing by the metal rod. The rope would pay out as I climbed; I left it coiled loosely on the ground. Gimenez braced himself against the wall and gave me a leg up. I stood on his shoulders, both hands gripping the rod, and tried to reach the edge of the skylight. I pulled myself up slowly, with all the strength I had. But it proved too much of an effort; I had to come down again.

The weeks of confinement I had undergone since my previous successful attempt must have sapped my strength more than I thought. We went back to the latrines to give me a few moments' rest. I inhaled deeply, waiting till I got my breath back before making a second attempt.

I had to get up there, whatever happened.

Jaws clenched, I began to climb. I got my feet from Gimenez's hands to his shoulders, and then to his head. My fingers gripped the metal rod convulsively. Somehow I went on, inch by inch; at last my fingers found the frame of the skylight, and I got my legs over the horizontal rod, which shook in its rings as my weight hung from it. I got round the ratchet supporting the skylight without touching it. I was sweating and panting like a man struggling out of a quicksand, or a shipwrecked sailor clinging desperately to a reef. Eyes dilated, every muscle cracking, I gradually worked my way through the opening. Then I stopped for a minute to get my strength back. I had managed to preserve absolute silence from start to finish.

A few lights twinkled in the distance. The fresh night air cooled my damp face. It was very still. Slowly my breathing became normal again. Carefully I put out one hand on to the gritty surface of the flat roof, taking care to avoid touching the fragile glass in the skylight itself; this done, I hauled myself up a little further and got my other hand into a similar position. With a final effort I completed the operation, and found myself standing upright on the roof, dazed by the clear splendour of the night sky. The silence drummed in my ears.

For a moment I remained motionless. Then I knelt down and slowly pulled up the rope. The shoes were dangling in their bundle at the end of it. I let it down again and brought up our coats. The third time I salvaged the big rope; it was a difficult job to squeeze it through the narrow opening.

Go slowly, I thought. Don't hurry. You've got plenty of time.

I unhooked the parcel and put it aside. Then I paid out the rope once more. We had agreed that Gimenez should tie it round his waist so that I could take up the slack and make his ascent easier. I waited a little, and then felt a gentle tug. I pulled steadily, hand over hand, taking care not to let the rope bear heavily on the metal edge of the skylight. We could not risk any noise. I heard the rods creaking under his weight; then, a moment later, two hands came up and got a grip on the sill. Slowly Gimenez's face and shoulders appeared.

I bent down and whispered: "Don't hurry. Take a rest."

He breathed in the fresh air, gulping and panting.

My mouth still close to his ear, I said: "Be careful how you pull yourself up. Don't put your hands on the glass."

He seemed as exhausted as I was.

I untied the rope from my waist, and he followed suit. I coiled it up carefully, took a piece of string out of my pocket, and ran a bowline round the middle of the coil.

There we both stood, side by side, in absolute silence. Gradually my breathing slowed down to its normal rate, and I began to recover my strength. It was hard to get used to this immense, seemingly limitless space all round me. The glass penthouse (of which the skylight formed a part) stood out from the roof and vanished in darkness only a few feet away. I made out one or two small chimney-cowls here and there. The courtyard and the perimeter were hidden from us by the parapet. We could walk upright without being seen.

I felt the shingle grit under my feet at the least move I made.

I took a coil of rope in each hand and picked them up with great care. Gimenez did the same with the shoes and coats. We stood there waiting for a train: it was five, perhaps even ten minutes coming.

Gimenez became impatient. I was just about to move when the

sound of a locomotive reached us from the distance. It grew louder and louder; presently the train steamed past on the nearby track. We managed to get ten feet forward before it vanished into the distance again. The stretch of line which runs past Montluc joins the two main stations of Lyons. As a result it carries very heavy traffic, which had hardly slackened off even at this stage of the war.

We had nearly reached the middle of the roof now. We found ourselves standing by the far end of the penthouse. A little further on a second penthouse appeared, which stretched away towards the other side of the roof. My eyes were beginning to get accustomed to the dark. I could see the large glass dome above the penthouse; that meant we were standing above the central well. I thought then for a moment of our friends below in their cells: some asleep, lost in wonderful dreams; others, who knew of our plan, awake, waiting in frightful suspense, ears straining for any suspicious noises.

We had advanced with extreme care, putting each foot down as lightly as possible, bent double as if the weight of our apprehension and of the dangers we had to face was too heavy to be supported. Gimenez kept close behind me. I could hear his slow, regular breathing, and glimpse his dark silhouette against the night sky. We had to wait some time before another train came to our assistance. But this time it was a slow goods train. It enabled us to reach our objective—the side of the roof opposite the infirmary—in one quick move.

We put down our various packages. I turned back and whispered to Gimenez: "Lie down and wait for me here. Don't move."

"Where are you going?"

"To see what's happening."

Gimenez obediently dropped to his knees, and remained as motionless as the equipment stacked round him. I crept slowly round the corner of the roof, raised myself cautiously, and peered over the parapet. Below me I could see the stretch of the perimeter which flanked the Rue du Dauphiné. I lifted my head a little further, and quickly drew it back again at the sight of a sentry. He was standing in one corner near the wash-house. I had known he would be there; yet in my present situation he scared me nearly out of my wits.

Of course, he could not see me. I told myself not to be a fool.

I pressed my cheek against the rough concrete surface and slowly raised my head once more. Unfortunately, the wide shelf outside the parapet cut off my view of the part of the courtyard immediately below. As this was where we would have to climb down, it was essential to find a better observation-post.

But before moving I took another quick look at the soldier in the far corner. He seemed very wide awake. Soon a second sentry walked over to join him—probably the one who guarded the wooden barrack-block on the other side. I saw the glowing tips of their cigarettes. The lamps in the courtyard gave off so weak a light that the men themselves were mere shadows against the surrounding gloom.

Occasionally a twinkling reflection from buckle or bayonet hinted at their movements. I knew that the best way of remaining unseen was to keep absolutely still. If I had to move, it must be done as slowly as possible, with long and frequent pauses. It took me some time to get back to Gimenez, tell him to stay put, climb over the parapet, and crawl along the outer cat-walk till I was once more opposite the infirmary. A train passed by at exactly the right moment; I scrambled along as fast as I could to the corner of the wall. A loose piece of shingle, even a little sand going over the edge would have given me away. I would feel ahead with my hands, then slowly pull myself forward like a slug, breathing through my mouth.

In front of me the perimeter was clearly visible. Beyond it the tobacco factory and the buildings of the military court formed a broken outline against the horizon. Above them the stars shone out in a moonless sky. After a little I could just make out the roof of the covered gallery over which we had to pass. Gradually our whole route became visible. I spotted a familiar landmark—the fanlight of my old cell—and then, on the left, the workshop and women's quarters. Close by was the low wall between the infirmary and the courtyard. Soon, I thought, we should be climbing that wall. One room in the infirmary was still lit up; the light shone behind the wall in the direction of the covered gallery. I was, I realised, directly above cell 45, where my first few weeks of detention had been spent.

I wriggled forward inch by inch, so as to reach the outer edge of the cat-walk and get into a position from which I could observe the whole area of the courtyard. The two sentries were now out of sight round the corner of the block, smoking and chatting. I could see no one below me. The way was clear. My heart beat excitedly. A little further and I would be certain. My face against the rough surface, I peered cautiously over the edge.

I was horrified at the gulf stretching down below me; I could not help feeling that my rope must be too short.

Nothing was stirring. I examined every danger-point in turn—the shadowy corners by the wash-house and workshop, the women's quarters, the alley between the infirmary wall and the main block, the half-open doors leading from court to court, every conceivable hole or corner where a sentry might be lurking. Nothing. The cell windows were patterned on the façade like black squares in a crossword puzzle. Occasionally the sound of a cough drifted out from one or other of them. This, and the recurrent trains, alone broke the silence. Further down, on the left, some of the windows seemed to be open. The stillness was almost tangible.

Still I scrutinised the courtyard with minute care. Suddenly a dark shape caught my eye, in a corner near the door of the main block. I stared closely at it. After a moment I realised it was a sentry, asleep on the steps. The weight of this alarming discovery filled me with a sudden vast depression. How on earth were we to get past him? How could we even be certain he was asleep? How—in the last resort—could we surprise him without being seen?

At this point the sentry sat up and lit a cigarette. The flame from his lighter gave me a quick glimpse of his steel helmet and the sub-machine gun he carried. He got up, walked a little way in the direction of the infirmary, and then came back again.

Midnight struck.

It must have been the time when the guard was changed. The

soldier passed directly beneath me, between the infirmary and the main block, and vanished in the direction of the guard-house. Four or five minutes later his relief appeared. His footsteps crunched grimly over the cobbles.

A frightful inner conflict racked me as I studied his every movement, like a wild beast stalking its prey. We could not retreat. The way had to be cleared.

The sentry's beat took him away into the shadows at the far end of the court, then back to the main door, where the lamp shone for a moment on his helmet and the barrel of his sub-machine gun.

I watched him for a whole hour, memorising the pattern of his movements. Then I raised myself on knees and elbows, climbed quietly over the parapet, and returned to Gimenez.

He was asleep. I woke him gently. "Time to move on," I said.

He got up without making any noise. I was busy untying the knot of the string lashed round the big rope.

"All set now," I whispered. "As soon as a train comes, we'll lower the rope."

I stood with one foot on the roof and the other on the cat-walk, the low parapet between my legs. This way I could control the rope with both hands and pay it out without it touching the edge. I left Gimenez to control the coil and see the rope was free from entanglements.

An eternity of time seemed to pass before the train came. At the first distant panting of the engine I began to lower away, slowly at first, then with increasing speed. When I felt the reinforced stretch near the end passing through my fingers I stopped, and lowered the rope on to the concrete. Then I hooked the grappling-iron on to the inner side of the parapet. It seemed to hold firm enough. The rope stretched away into the darkness below us.

Gimenez would sling the parcels containing our shoes and coats round his neck, and follow me down when I gave him the signal. I knew that the moment I swung out from the roof into open space the last irrevocable decision would have been taken. By so doing I would either clinch my victory or sign my own death-warrant. While I remained on the roof it was still possible to return to my cell. Once I had begun the descent there was no way back. Despite the cool night air, my face and shirt were soaked with sweat.

"Hold on to the grappling-iron while I'm going down," I told Gimenez. I took hold of his hands and set them in position.

Then I crouched down on the outer ledge, facing him, ready to go down the rope at the first possible moment, and waited for a train to pass. Gimenez leant over and hissed nervously in my ear: "There's someone down below!"

"Don't worry."

Then I looked at the sky and the stars and prayed that the rope might be strong enough, that the German sentry would not come round the corner at the wrong moment, that I would not make any accidental noise.

The waiting strained my nerves horribly. Once I began my descent there would be no more hesitation, I knew; but dear God, I thought, let that train come quickly, let me begin my descent into the abyss now, at once, before my strength fails me.

The stroke of one o'clock cut through the stillness like an axe.

Had an hour passed so quickly? The sentries' footsteps, echoing up to us with monotonous regularity, seemed to be counting out the seconds. There could not be so very many trains at this time of night.

Gimenez was showing signs of impatience. I told him to keep still. The words were hardly out of my mouth when a distant whistle broke the silence. Quickly it swelled in volume.

"This is it," I said.

I shuffled back towards the edge of the cat-walk. Then, holding my breath, I slid myself over, gripping the rope between my knees, and holding the ledge with both hands to steady myself. At last I let go. The rope whirred upwards under my feet, the wire binding tore at my hands. I went down as fast as I could, not even using my legs.

As soon as I touched the ground I grabbed the parcel containing the second rope, and doubled across the courtyard to the low wall. I released the rope, swung the grappling iron up, hauled myself over, and dropped down on the other side, behind the doorway, leaving the rope behind for Gimenez.

The train was fading away into the distance now, towards the station. The drumming of its wheels seemed to be echoed in my heaving chest. I opened my mouth and breathed deeply to ease the pressure on my lungs. Above me I saw the dark swinging line of rope, and the sharp outline of the roof against the sky.

I stood motionless, getting my breath back and accustoming my eyes to the darkness. The sentry's footsteps rang out behind the wall, scarcely six feet away. They passed on, only to return a moment later. I pressed both hands against my beating heart. When all was quiet again I worked round to the doorway, and flattened myself against it. I felt all my human reactions being swallowed up by pure animal instinct, the instinct for self-preservation which quickens the reflexes and gives one fresh reserves of strength.

It was my life or his.

As his footsteps approached I tried to press myself into the wood against which my back was resting. Then, when I heard him change direction, I risked a quick glance out of my hiding-place to see exactly where he was.

He did exactly the same thing twice, and still I waited.

I got a good grip on the ground with my heels; I could not afford to slip. The footsteps moved in my direction, grew louder. The sentry began to turn . . .

I sprang out of my recess like a panther, and got my hands round his throat in a deadly grip. With frantic violence I began to throttle him. I was no longer a man, but a wild animal. I squeezed and squeezed, with the terrible strength of desperation. My teeth were gritting against each other, my eyes bursting out of my head. I threw back my head to exert extra pressure, and felt my fingers bite deep into his neck. Already half-strangled, the muscles of his throat torn and engorged, only held upright by my vice-like grip, the sentry still feebly raised his arms as if to defend himself; but an instant later they fell back, inert. But this did not make me let go. For perhaps three minutes longer I maintained my pressure on his throat, as if afraid that one last cry, or even the death-rattle, might give me away. Then, slowly, I loosened my blood-stained fingers, ready to close them again at the least movement; but the body remained slack and lifeless. I lowered it gently to the ground.

I stared down at the steel helmet which, fortunately perhaps, concealed the sentry's face; at the dark hunched shape of the body itself, at the sub-machine gun and the bayonet. I thought for a moment, then quickly drew the bayonet from its scabbard, gripped it by the hilt in both hands, and plunged it down with one straight, hard stroke into the sentry's back.

I raised my head, and saw that I was standing immediately below the window of cell 45. Old memories fireworked up in my mind: hunger and thirst, the beatings I had suffered, the handcuffs, the condemned man in the next cell, Fränzel spitting in my face.

My revenge had begun.

I went back to the doorway, near the infirmary, and whistled twice, very softly. A dark shape slid down the rope. It creaked under his weight. I went to meet him. Gimenez climbed the low wall, detached the light rope with its grappling-iron, passed them down to me, and jumped. In his excitement, or nervousness, he had left our coats and shoes on the roof. At the time I said nothing about this. Clearly his long wait had depressed him; he was shivering all over. He gave a violent start when he saw the corpse stretched out near our feet.

I clapped him on the back. "You'll really have something to shiver about in a moment. Come on, quick."

Our troubles had only begun. We still had to cross the courtyard in order to reach the wall between it and the infirmary. Then there was the roof of the covered gallery to surmount, and, finally, the crossing of the perimeter walls.

I carried the rope and the fixed grappling-iron; Gimenez had the loose one. We doubled across to the wall. It was essential for us to get up here as quickly as possible. The light left on in the infirmary was shining in our direction, and a guard could easily have spotted us from a first-floor window of the central block as we made our way towards the inner wall of the perimeter.

Gimenez gave me a leg up, and I managed to reach the top of the wall and hang on. But I was quite incapable by now of pulling myself up; all my strength had drained away. I came down again, wiped my forehead and regained my breath. If I had been alone I should in all probability have stuck at this point. As it was I bent down against the wall in my turn, and Gimenez got up without any trouble. I undid the bundle of rope and passed him the end with the grappling-iron attached. He fixed it securely. Then I tried again, with the rope to help me this time. Somehow I scrambled up, using hands, knees and feet, thrusting and straining in one last desperate effort. Gimenez lay down flat on his belly to give himself more purchase, and managed to grasp me under the arms. Eventually I made it.

My heart was hammering against my ribs and my chest felt as if it was going to burst. My shirt clung damply to my body. But there was not a minute to lose. We coiled up the rope again and crawled along to the covered gallery. From here it was a short climb up the tiles to the ridge of the roof. We had to hurry because of that damned light; once we had got over the other side of the roof we were in shadow again.

Unfortunately I made a noise. Two tiles knocked against each other under the sliding pressure of my knee. Gimenez reproved me sharply.

"For God's sake take care what you're doing!" he hissed.

"It wasn't my fault—"

"I haven't the least desire to be caught, even if you have!"

Since this was a sloping roof, we only needed to climb a little way down the far side to be completely hidden. If we stood upright we could easily see over the wall. Soon we were both crouching in position at the end of the covered gallery, our equipment beside us.

I was not acquainted with the exact details of the patrols in the perimeter. When I went out to be interrogated, I had observed a sentry-box in each corner, but these were always unoccupied. Perhaps the guards used them at night, however: it was vital to find out. We already knew that one guard rode round and round the whole time on a bicycle; he passed us every two or three minutes, his pedals squeaking.

We listened carefully. Gimenez was just saying that the cyclist must be alone when the sound of voices reached us. We had to think again.

Perhaps there was a sentry posted at each corner of the square, in the angle formed by the outer wall. If this turned out to be so, it would be extremely difficult to get across; nothing but complete darkness would give us a chance. That meant we must cut the electric cable, which ran about two feet below the top of the inner wall, on the perimeter side.

I half-rose from my cramped position and took a quick look. The walls seemed much higher from here, and the lighting system enhanced this impression. A wave of despair swept over me. Surely we could never surmount this obstacle?

From the roof it had all looked very different. The yawning gulf had been hidden. But the perimeter was well-lit, and the sight of it—deep as hell and bright as daylight—almost crushed my exhausted determination.

I craned forward a little further. The sentry-box below on our left was empty. I ducked back quickly as the cyclist approached. He ground round the corner and started another circuit. A moment later I was enormously relieved to hear him talking to himself; it was this curious monologue we had intercepted a moment earlier. He was alone, after all.

Behind us rose the dark shape of the main block. We had come a long way since ten o'clock. Another six yards, and we were free. Yet what risks still remained to be run!

Little by little determination flowed back into me. One more effort would do it. Don't look back, I thought. Keep your eyes in front of you till it's all over.

Bitter experience had taught me that over-hastiness could be fatal; that every precipitate action was liable to bring disaster in its train. Gimenez was eager to get on and finish the operation, but I firmly held him back. I was as well aware as he was of the dangers that threatened us; I knew that every moment we delayed increased our risk of recapture. I thought of the open cell, the rope we had left hanging from the wall, the dead sentry in the court-yard, the possibility of his body being discovered by a patrol or his relief. Nevertheless, I spent more than a quarter of an hour watching that cyclist. Every four or five circuits he turned round and went the other way. We were well-placed in our corner: he was busy taking the bend, and never looked up. We were additionally protected by the three shaded lights fixed on each wall. All their radiance was thrown down into the perimeter itself, leaving us in shadow. We could watch him without fear of discovery.

Three o'clock.

Gimenez was becoming desperate. At last I decided to move. Holding the end of the rope firmly in one hand, I coiled it across my left arm like a lasso. With the other hand I grasped the grappling-iron. As soon as the sentry had pedalled past, I threw the line as hard as I could towards the opposite wall. The rope snaked up and out, and the grappling-iron fell behind the parapet. I tugged very gently on it, trying to let it find a natural anchorage. Apparently I had been successful; it held firm. A strand of barbed wire, which I had not previously noticed, rattled alarmingly as the rope jerked over it. After a little, however, it was pressed down to the level of the wall.

I gave one violent pull, but the rope did not budge. It had caught first time. I breathed again.

"Give me the other hook," I muttered to Gimenez. I could feel him trembling.

The cyclist was coming round again now. I froze abruptly. For the first time he passed actually under the rope. When he had gone I threaded the rope through the wire loop and pulled it as tight as we could. While Gimenez held it firm to prevent it slipping, I knotted it tightly, and fixed the grappling-iron in a crevice on the near side of the parapet. In my fear of running things too fine I had actually overcalculated the amount of rope necessary; over six feet were left trailing loose on the roof. That thin line stretching across the perimeter looked hardly less fragile than the telephone-wires which followed a similar route a few yards away.

I made several further tests when the cyclist was round the other side. I unanchored the grappling-iron on our side, and then we both of us pulled on the rope as hard as we could to try out its strength.

If the truth must be told, I was horribly afraid that it would snap, and I would be left crippled in the perimeter. When I pulled on it with all my strength I could feel it stretch. One last little effort and the whole thing would be over; but I had reached the absolute end of my courage, physical endurance, and will-power alike. All the time the cyclist continued to ride round beneath us.

Four o'clock struck.

In the distance, towards the station, the red lights on the railway line still shone out. But the first glimmer of dawn was already creeping up over the horizon, and the lights showed less bright every moment. We could wait no longer.

"Over you go, Gimenez. You're lighter than I am."

"No. You go first."

"It's your turn."

"I won't."

"Go on, it's up to you."

"No," he said desperately, "I can't do it."

The cyclist turned the corner again. I shook Gimenez desperately, my fingers itching to hit him.

"Are you going, yes or no?"

"No," he cried, "no, *no!*"

"Shut up, for God's sake!" I said. I could not conquer his fear; I said no more. Still the German pedalled round his beat. Once he stopped almost directly beneath us, got off his machine, and urinated against the wall. It was at once a comic and terrifying sight. As time passed and the dawn approached, our chances of success grew steadily less. I knew it, yet I still hesitated. Gimenez shivered in silence.

Abruptly, as the sentry passed us yet again, I stooped forward, gripped the rope with both hands, swung out into space, and got my legs up into position. Hand over hand, my back hanging exposed above the void, I pulled myself across with desperate speed. I reached the far wall, got one arm over it, and scrambled up.

I had done it. I had escaped.

A delirious feeling of triumph swept over me. I forgot how exhausted I was; I almost forgot Gimenez, who was still waiting for the sentry to pass under him again before following me. I was oblivious to my thudding heart and hoarse breath; my knees might tremble, my face be dripping with sweat, my hands scored and bleeding, my throat choked, my head bursting, but I neither knew nor cared. All I was conscious of was the smell of life, the freedom I had won against such desperate odds. I uttered a quick and thankful prayer to God for bringing me through safely.

I moved along the top of the wall towards the courthouse buildings, where it lost height considerably. I stopped just short of a small gateway. Workmen were going past in the street outside, and I waited a few moments before jumping down. This gave Gimenez time to catch up with me.

At five o'clock we were walking down the street in our socks and shirt-sleeves—free men.

We wanted to shout out loud with joy, to run, dance, go completely mad. Never till now had I understood the full force and meaning of the word *freedom*.

We made off in what I guessed to be the direction of Villeurbanne. We walked rapidly through the deserted streets; the town was still asleep. I had no very clear idea where we were, but my instinct told me that the one important thing was to put as much distance between us and Montluc as possible.

All the time we talked and talked, in an uncontrollable spate of words.

"Gimenez, Giminez, we've done the impossible!" I said.

"If my mother could see me now!"

"When Fränzel discovers the open cell, and the ropes, and the dead sentry—"

"And the dismantled bed, and our shoes and coats on the roof—"

"What the hell did you leave them behind for?" I asked.

"I was so scared I forgot them."

I could not be angry now. "No more straw mattresses . . ."

"And no more cells."

"Or lice," I said, with some feeling.

"They'll send Fränzel to the Russian front for this."

"Or the glasshouse."

Gimenez said: "You were right, over everything."

"Yes, I was right. But it's only now I know I was."

We walked on tirelessly.

I said: "We ought to separate, Gimenez. It'd be safer."

"Why?"

"Because in an hour at most they'll find we're gone, and start looking for us."

"No," he said obstinately, "I'm staying with you."

"Don't you understand? It doubles the risk of being caught. We'd do far better on our own."

"It's no good. I'm not going to leave you. You promised to take care of me, didn't you?"

It was no use arguing. We went on our way in silence. The fresh morning air cooled my face, and I gulped it greedily into my lungs. Elated, I gazed at the free world that stretched out before us. I was drunk with my success.

Mere physical weakness—numb muscles, stiff and feeble joints —meant nothing. The human body possesses infinite powers on which the basic instinct for self-preservation can always draw.

It was almost completely light now. We would have to knock at a door, any door, and ask for help. Several times already we had had to turn off down a side road to avoid encountering passers-by, who would almost certainly have found our appearance highly suspicious. On we went, the pavement granite-hard under our shoeless feet. But all the doors were shut.

"Come on, Gimenez. We've got to go further yet."

I had no idea where we were; we had been turning from one street to another completely at random. Then, suddenly, I caught sight of a street-sign which read: Boulevard des Belges. But I had a friend here, of course, at No. 92. Dr. Bacharach.

"Gimenez," I said, "we're saved. This way. Quick."

It was broad daylight when we reached the big block of flats. We went quickly up the stairs to the first floor and I rang the front-door bell.

Nothing happened.

"Supposing they're away?" Gimenez asked.

"Wait a minute."

I pressed the button again, and heard the bell ringing inside. Then muffled footsteps approached the door, and a man's voice called out: "Who's that?"

"Valentine," I said, giving my code-name.

The doctor opened the door and stood there dumb with surprise, mouth wide open.

I said: "I escaped from Montluc early this morning. I have brought another prisoner with me. His name is Gimenez."

"Come in quickly, both of you."

Dr. Bacharach's flat was decorated and furnished with most exquisite taste. We must have looked like two alley-cats in a glass cabinet.

"Do you recognise me, Doctor?" I asked.

He smiled. "Just about. Come into the kitchen. I must go and wake my secretary and slip on a dressing-gown."

Gimenez was watching me anxiously.

"Is there something troubling you?" I asked him.

"I thought you might be angry with me for not going across the rope first. I was afraid to."

"No, of course not," I said. "It was my own stupidity. I ought to have gone on myself without waiting. We should have gained an hour that way. Anyway, the main thing is that we're out, and in safe hands."

He nodded.

The doctor's secretary, Mme. Lonjaret, was just as surprised as the doctor himself.

"What a state you're in!" she said, and at once set about preparing hot coffee and cutting bread-and-butter. Gimenez watched her activities with ill-disguised pleasure.

I asked the doctor what the time was.

"Six o'clock."

"Six o'clock? It's getting late. The Germans'll soon discover everything—our ropes, the dead sentry, the cell door. They probably have already. There's bound to be a wonderful hullabaloo in Montluc today."

He said: "It's incredible that you managed to get away at all. The place is an absolute fortress."

"A desperate man can perform miracles. There was no other way. A chance in a million against certain death, but the one chance was worth fighting for."

"Ponchardier told me you had been arrested, in April. He came to warn me. I burnt every document in my possession at once."

"Did the Gestapo follow the trail back to you?"

"No," said Dr. Bacharach, "they didn't. But I did have a highly suspicious visitor soon after you had been imprisoned. A man claiming to be one of our agents from Toulouse. He was anxious to find out all he could about you. I led him up the garden in fine style."

I asked him what had been happening since April.

"The usual sort of thing. Nothing's changed much. Talafre and Muller still come in to pick up messages and pass them on. The organisation's still working efficiently. By the way, how did that little affair of yours in Nice go off? I remember giving you some chloroform you said you wanted—"

"As a matter of fact I never used it. I killed the Italian officer, though. It all went according to plan. I was arrested three days later, on April 17. A Gestapo agent had managed to get into the organisation somehow."

Gimenez was wolfing down his breakfast with an appetite that clearly took Mme. Lonjaret somewhat aback. But he had not missed a word of our conversation.

"You killed an Italian officer?" he asked.

"Yes. He had done us a great deal of harm."

At my request the doctor gave us a brief account of the latest events at the front. We heard about El Alamein, Tobruk, and Bir Hakeim, the landings in Italy, and the Russian campaign.

My questions astonished him. He said: "Didn't you get any news in prison? Weren't there any papers?"

"A few rumours passed on from one cell to the next, that's all. And always inaccurate."

He set about looking out clothes and shoes for us both.

"We won't have any trouble with your friend," he said, looking Gimenez up and down. "I'm almost exactly the same height and build as he is. I doubt whether I've got anything that'll fit you, though."

Gimenez was quickly dealt with. He wore one of the doctor's sports jackets, which fitted him perfectly, and a beautiful pair of mountaineer's shoes. For me, Bacharach enlisted the help of the hall-porter, who produced a serviceable pair of espadrilles. After several attempts I managed to struggle into one of the doctor's old coats. There were no limits to his generosity.

What sort of appearance would I present? Somewhat alarming, I suspected. My trousers were torn and threadbare; my coat was too tight, and its sleeves much too short. I stank horribly, my face was ashy pale, my hair tangled and badly cut, and my expression highly furtive.

What were we going to do? The peace and quiet of this flat were highly tempting. We might perhaps have stayed there a little, but it would have been exceedingly rash. I wondered who the man was who had visited the doctor after my arrest. It occurred to me that he was capable of making a good deal of trouble for my friends.

I had, besides, an almost irresistible urge to get out into the countryside. There was no doubt about it, that was what we must do. I was convinced that we could be more easily concealed in the country villages. Gradually, by short stages, we could reach Savoy, and then cross the frontier into Switzerland.

I repeated to the doctor the arguments with which I had earlier tried to convince Gimenez, saying it would be much safer from every point of view if we went separately. "If we stay here," I said, "we shall be putting you in a very dangerous position. Supposing the police raided the flat: they'd arrest the lot of us. We've got to get out of town. It's here they'll start looking for us."

"Perhaps you're right," Bacharach said. "There's a tram you could catch just outside, near the station, number 27. That would take you as far as Croix-Luizet. After that you ought to be able to make your own way on foot without much danger."

I thanked him gratefully. "Would you do one more thing for me?" I asked.

"Of course. Anything you want."

"Will you send a telegram to my parents?"

"I'd be glad to."

I scribbled down a message. It read: *Out of hospital stop fear infection stop take all precautions—André*. I hoped they would understand the hint, and get away as soon as possible.

Clothed, fed, refreshed, with money in our pockets, we walked off in the direction of the station.

This walk between Bacharach's flat and the tram terminus was pure agony. We thought every passer-by recognised us at once; "Escaped Prisoner" seemed to be written all over our faces. I felt curiously intoxicated, drunk with apprehension, fresh air, freedom and sheer exhaustion.

The square in front of the station was already full of bustle and life. Crowds of pedestrians, both men and women, were hurrying to and fro, cars and buses sped past. I suddenly felt that the life I had left five months before had at last become a reality once again. The trees were thick with leaves, the air was warm. Was it all a dream? I felt that at any moment I would wake up and find myself in my cell, listening to the familiar banging and shouting. I rubbed my eyes to make sure I was awake.

We found the tram-stop for Croix-Luizet without much difficulty. Before we caught the tram I said once more to Gimenez: "We would do better to travel separately. Take this tram or the next. I don't mind waiting."

"No, I can't leave you. You promised to see me through this business."

"That was when we were in prison. You had to follow me then. It's a different matter now we're outside."

"My mind's made up, André. I'm going with you."

There was an expression of hurt reproachfulness on his face: he looked like a kicked dog. I could not help feeling sorry for him.

"All right," I said. "You can come with me."

12

I found it impossible to concentrate on the paper I had bought. Throughout the journey we never once dared to look up. We were automatically suspicious of every traveller in the bus; we saw enemy agents everywhere. The most harmless peasant took on a hangman's air. We got down at the terminus, and then, without even stopping to ask the way, set off out of the town as fast as we could.

I told Gimenez to hurry. "We can relax in open country," I said. "No houses, no inquisitive people, and some hide-out where we can rest. Sleep, my God, how I want to sleep! I'm absolutely worn out. My head's going round."

"Let's keep on for a bit. Look, if we cross this big bridge, and get past that village over there, we can stop anywhere outside."

But at that moment I caught sight of a company of German soldiers engaged on a field-exercise. There were numbers of them spread across the fields on both sides of our route. The sight abruptly restored my energy.

"What are they up to?" Gimenez asked.

"I'm not sure." But then I caught sight of trucks and artillery, and several columns marching in close order. "Manœuvres," I explained.

190

Gimenez quickened his pace, contenting himself with the observation that this was a fine time for them to start training.

"Don't hurry," I told him. "Don't give any sign that they disturb you. All we have to do is walk on steadily towards those houses over there."

Mile after mile we trudged on. A numbing lassitude crept over me. Every moment I felt more desperately in need of rest and sleep. Only the joy I felt at my new-found freedom, the unlooked-for delight of once more being in the country, among green, sweet-smelling trees, following a road that wound away to the distant horizon —only these things kept me going. I had been deprived of them for too long, and discovered them again with almost agonising pleasure. Without the impetus they gave me—sharpened, to be sure, by those figures in field-grey uniform moving about the fields—I should have gone to sleep there and then by the roadside.

"Once you lay down you'd never get up again," Gimenez said. "You look all in."

I came to the conclusion I must be in a bad way. The doctor had only just recognized me, and now this boy was telling me I looked all in. I could hardly feel my legs moving. But I would not stop now. I had to keep straight on. I thought of poor Jeantet; he must know by now that I had got away. I was glad I had not failed him; I only hoped he would not suffer for all the help he had given me.

Gimenez asked me why I was muttering to myself. He looked worried; I must, without knowing it, have been speaking my thoughts aloud.

"Nothing, it's nothing," I said. "My head's feeling a bit queer, that's all."

Gimenez said: "Here's a farm."

"Wait here a moment. I can see someone inside. I'll go and ask them for help."

We had reached the village of Vaux-en-Velin. I went into the courtyard and called out to the labourer I had seen.

"Have you got a map of this area?"

He looked us up and down; then said, slowly: "No, there's no map here. But you can get hold of one easily enough."

"Where?"

"Ask the Mayor. He lives down the road there."

This was to invite suspicion. Accordingly I said: "Oh, it's not all that important. We won't bother. Just tell us if we're in the right direction for Savoy."

He thought for a moment.

"Savoy. Let's see. You've got to cross the Rhone, that's certain. See that spinney over there? The river's beyond it. When you get there, shout out for the ferryman. He lives on the other side. You can ask him the way."

We thanked him, and set off along a lane which led through the fields. The labourer watched us as we went, and then slouched off, muttering to himself. What on earth were these two tramps after, with all their talk about a map? Savoy, indeed! Vagabonds, probably thieves . . .

Our path took us through deep, lush meadows; on our right a line of trees marked the course of the river. The thick dust filled my tattered espadrilles. There were no German soldiers anywhere to be seen now.

"We're alone at last, Gimenez," I said. "Once we've crossed the Rhone we're going to stop at the first house we come to and ask them to put us up. I can't go on any further."

"I'm tired out myself," Gimenez admitted. "Once we're across the river we'll be all right."

Now we were passing through a thick belt of trees. Sometimes branching willows brushed across our faces. We came out on a shore of sloping shingle. Beyond it the river flowed green and clear between thickly wooded banks.

I gazed at the scene in front of me; the peaceful river, magnificent in its wild quietness; the tangled thickets, the crisp shingle. I felt that here we should find the peace we so desperately needed.

The ferryman's cottage was just visible among the trees on the far bank. With its whitewashed walls, red-tiled roof, and bright, flowering garden it seemed an ideal haven for us. These warm, vivid colours were enriched still more by the sunlight in which they were bathed.

"Give him a call, Gimenez!"

His voice echoed out over the still water. Nothing stirred. After a moment he shouted again.

A woman appeared from the cottage, walked down to the bank, cast off in a flat-bottomed boat and rowed across to us. We got in beside her. I felt suddenly and unbelievably happy.

The woman was still young, and glowing with health. As she tugged at the oars she eyed us with some astonishment, but not unpleasantly. We stepped out on the far bank. Gimenez helped her to moor the boat; then we all three climbed up the steps from the landing-stage.

In front of us a little terrace set with chairs and tables beckoned invitingly.

I asked her if they ran a café here.

"Indeed we do; a restaurant, in fact."

"Could we sit down for a little?"

"Of course."

I found a seat in the sun. Would we like something to drink? I asked her what there was.

"Beer, wine, coffee—"

"You say this is a restaurant?"

"Yes."

"Got anything to eat?"

"It's not easy these days," she said. "But I've got some sausages and eggs—"

"You could make us an omelette, then?"

"Oh yes. How many eggs would you like in it?"

"What do you think, Gimenez?"

"I don't know. Just as you like."

"Right," I said. "A dozen ought to do us."

"A *dozen?*" The woman was really amazed now.

"Don't be alarmed. I'll explain the situation. You look a nice

sort of girl. I'm sure we can trust you. We're escaped prisoners—
just got away from the Germans."

"Where?"

"Montluc," I said.

"My God!"

"We're absolutely dead-beat and ravenously hungry. We've got a
little money, but no ration-books. After that nightmare existence
this cottage is like Paradise. You can have no idea what sort of place
Montluc is." I looked around me. "Sunlight and fresh air, all these
trees, the river—it's too good to be true—"

She shook her head in sympathy. "I'll get you something right
away," she said.

I turned to Gimenez and went on: "Yesterday we were in hell.
Now we're free to enjoy all this natural beauty—free, free! Can you
feel the sun on your back, Gimenez? Do you realise what extraordinary luck we've had? There's a wonderful time ahead of us. First,
we'll go home and see our parents—"

He nodded eagerly.

". . . And our friends—"

He said vehemently: "I want to be with you wherever you go."

"Don't worry. Listen—don't say anything! Listen to the birds,
and the running water, and the leaves rustling! Oh, God, how wonderful it is to be in the country again!"

I broke off short, in sudden terror. The nightmare had returned.
My blood went cold; I felt as if I would choke. I put one hand on
Gimenez's leg, ready to run for it. A file of five German soldiers had
suddenly appeared on the river bank, about twenty yards off, and
were making straight for us.

I managed to say: "Don't move. Go on talking."

They halted close to our table, and a sergeant said, in excellent
French: "Your papers, please."

"Papers? What papers?" I replied. "We haven't got them with
us. We're just country folk. We work as painters on a farm near
here. We've just come in here for a drink."

"You have no means of identification?"

"You know how it is," I said. "You don't carry papers around with you when you're working."

"Come with us, please."

While the astonished woman looked on—and in spite of our vehement protestations—he took us off under escort. The ground seemed to have opened up under my feet.

Good-bye now to this magnificent countryside, the noble river and bright sunlight; what sins had I committed to be so cruelly punished? If God had snatched me from that living tomb only to plunge me back into it a few hours later, why could He not have left me there, and not mocked my desperation in this way?

I marched between my captors like an automaton, without seeing them. After about a hundred yards we reached an open space near the river, where a number of vehicles were drawn up. I immediately noticed a wireless-truck among them. A large number of troops were busily occupied here. I realised that this must be the command-post of some unit or other; obviously we had been moving through an area set aside for manœuvres. The sergeant who had arrested us had a few quick words with an officer. The officer walked up to us, examined us carefully, and stopped short after one look at my face. He barked out an order.

A soldier told us, in French, to follow him.

Escorted by two men, we went back over the ground we had just covered. A little way down the path I decided to risk asking them where they were taking us.

One of them said: "Back to your work."

"Fine."

We went past the café and then, without asking permission got into the boat. The soldiers followed us. Gimenez took the oars and we rowed across the river.

Get away, a voice whispered in my head, get away now, don't hesitate. Run, quickly. Keep the initiative.

The words repeated themselves over and over again, in a kind of mad refrain. I looked at our escort, then at the water, the river-banks, and the sky. Gimenez, astonishingly unperturbed despite the strange position he found himself in, was struggling silently against the current. At last we got out and pulled the boat ashore. It ground over the shingle like a coffin. We struck out on a foot-path that wound away into the trees. Gimenez went first, with the sergeant and private following him; I brought up the rear.

I dawdled along, trying to spin out time before, inevitably, I should be forced to act.

How could we attack both of them at once? If only I could rely on Gimenez, I thought. Trip them both up, grab their pistols and bayonets, and then, without a second's hesitation—

Don't hesitate, the voice said. Run, quickly. Another moment and it'll be too late.

The sergeant and Gimenez had drawn a little way ahead. They were out in the open now, beyond the thicket, and were cutting across the meadow to pick up the path again at a corner which was just visible in the distance. The soldier was about twelve yards in front of me; he was following them without once looking back.

I took a quick jump to the left, off the track, and plunged into the thicket, dodging from bush to bush. I crossed one bridle-path, then another. Lacerated by thorns, branches springing back in my face, stumbling over roots and struggling desperately through dense undergrowth, I ran like a madman, my one aim to put as much distance between myself and the two soldiers as possible. When I reached the river I stripped off my coat, plunged in, and swam across to the other side. I slipped through a curtain of weeping willow that hung down into the water, and crouched there in the mud.

I was horribly out of breath, and it took some time for the hammering in my chest to die down. About two hundred yards downstream I could see the ferry-boat crossing the river again. There were three men in it.

Poor Gimenez, I thought; would he, one day, forgive me for abandoning him?

Fate, I thought, had treated me abominably. What was I to do now? It did not take me long to convince myself that Gimenez had talked—that he had admitted our identity as prisoners escaped from Montluc. Numerous patrols of three or four men began to move up and down the banks of the river, beating the undergrowth and bushes as they went. Some came dangerously near the place where I was hidden. But exactly as on the previous evening, when I had surprised and strangled the sentry, my instinct once again took over from my reason. Once again I behaved like a hunted animal.

I remained absolutely still, barely breathing.

On both sides of me I heard the voices of my pursuers growing louder. They were conducting their search in a highly methodical fashion, and looked as if they would join up somewhere near my retreat. There was a crackling of broken branches, and the squelch of feet in the damp earth. I peered through a gap in the thick river-grass, and saw several soldiers so close to me that I literally held my breath for fear of discovery. They moved slowly about, stooping down to see if they could find my tracks on the bank. It is hard to describe the terror I experienced at that moment. I must have found life infinitely desirable to go through such vicissitudes to preserve it.

Their friends called out to them, and the group of soldiers lounged off, talking as they went. When they had gone, I set about scraping out a hole in the muddy, overhanging bank in which I could conceal myself more securely. As I silently scooped out each handful of silt I kept repeating the magic words to myself: One last effort and you'll be safe.

But since the previous evening I had so exhausted myself that now even this black, soft viscous mud seemed as heavy as lead.

Hour after hour I lay there, concealed by the rank grass overhanging the river, up to my waist in filthy, muddy water. My strength and courage were at their last ebb. I would have been incapable of defending myself if I had been discovered; they could have shot me down on the spot, and I would have made no move to stop them. I felt myself the helpless victim of Fate, without the will to struggle any longer against the inevitable.

Beyond my hiding-place the river ran cool and clear, chuckling round buried roots and tugging gently at the branches that trailed in the water.

Once again I could listen to the birds singing. Sometimes a trout surfaced, and snapped up a stray gnat. Sometimes a swallow skimmed along the water's edge, flicking up over the bushes like a flash of light.

From time to time I cupped my hands and drank down great gulps of river-water; it was wonderfully cool and refreshing. I also rinsed the mud and sweat from my face. Slowly, without making any movement that might have given me away, I worked myself into a more comfortable position, up on the bank itself. I removed my espadrilles and wrung out my socks. Beneath the thick undergrowth it was warm and shady. I began to feel better.

I was completely worn out. My heavy eyelids closed; my breathing became slow and regular. My situation might be desperate, but I could no longer worry about it. Almost immediately I fell into a deep sleep.

The sun was high in the heavens when I awoke. My eyelids were swollen and tacky; I had a splitting headache. I had half-slipped back into the water while I was asleep. It was essential to find a more comfortable retreat. The mosquitoes had attacked me with some zest; I was bitten all over. They still whined round me in dense, angry swarms.

It was about three o'clock, perhaps more. The long sleep had refreshed me and renewed my energy.

The river had lost its blueness, but still ran quiet and clear. Once more I stared in delighted amazement at the magnificent scenery which had replaced those grey walls, the tiny barred window, the thick, imprisoning door. The air was clean and untainted; I was no longer shut off from the sky. I was astounded by the grace and beauty of the natural world, and all my senses were surfeited by the sheer intensity of colour, the orchestra of sounds which nature offers.

About thirty yards down-river, on the other bank, I saw a thick clump of weeping willows which might afford me a new hiding-place. I felt a desperate and irresistible urge to move, no matter where. After taking a good look at the surrounding countryside, I slipped into the water and swam lazily across, letting the current carry me down. I gripped a trailing branch and hauled myself up on to the bank. I stood for a moment letting the water drip off my clothes, wringing out my shirt and drying my face.

Then I walked slowly and cautiously towards the edge of the thicket I had chosen. In the marshy land round Vaux-en-Velin the thickets grow so rank and dense that it is almost impossible to find anyone in them. Despite everything, I had had this one piece of luck. I forced my way through a tangle of undergrowth. Slowly it thinned out, and I found myself at its furthest edge. The fields stretched away in front of me to the horizon.

I settled down in a convenient hiding-place, and scanned the countryside carefully. It was deserted. Like a sniper at his post, I tried to find some trace of life, anything to occupy my attention and stop me falling asleep once more. My clothes gradually dried on me, and the heat penetrated my cold and sodden body.

Suddenly I heard a noise of footsteps on my left. A man emerged from a path through the wood, pushing a bicycle. He stopped and looked out over the fields. Then he leant his bicycle against a bush, took a sickle out of a bag, and began to cut the tall grass, stuffing it into the bag in handfuls as he did so.

God must have sent him, I thought. I did not know how near the truth I was.

His age, expression and general appearance at once inspired me with confidence. There is, without doubt, an instinct in human beings which can distinguish friend from enemy. I whistled softly.

He paused, trying to make out where the sound had come from.

"This way. Over here," I whispered.

Still slashing away at the grass, he worked his way over towards me, till we were face to face. He started with amazement when he saw me, and blurted out: "Are you the man they're looking for?"

"Yes, I'm the man. I escaped last night."

"They're searching the village at this very moment, and interrogating all the inhabitants. I was stopped by a patrol on my way here."

I said: "You don't know me, but I am a French officer. I'm at the end of my tether. I've just spent five months in Montluc Prison. I had a terrible time escaping."

"You escaped from Montluc!" he said, amazed.

"Like a fool I let myself be picked up again here this morning, but I got away. I can't go on. I'm worn out."

He immediately said, without a moment's hesitation: "You are going to come to my house in Lyons. 29, Rue Massena."

Every line of his face showed generosity and frankness. His expression was open, direct. I felt certain he meant what he said.

Nevertheless I said: "Can I trust you?"

"Yes, you can trust me. Mind you remember my name and address."

He took out his identity card and gave it to me. It said his name was Jean Trombert, and that he was born at Essert-Homans in Haute-Savoie.

"So you're a Savoyard," I said.

"I am indeed; but I've been living in Lyons for thirty years now."

"I come from the same area myself—Habère-Lullin, in the Boëge Valley."

"I know the place. What an extraordinary coincidence! Do you know, this is the first time I've ever come here? I was after grass for my rabbits."

I asked if I should go back with him.

"Not now, it's out of the question. You'll have to wait till nightfall. It would be far too risky for us to be seen together."

He looked at the mud encrusted on my trousers, my torn, stained shirt, and my bare feet. Then he said: "I'll be waiting for you tonight, outside my front door."

"Where is the Rue Massena?"

"Go back past the village here as far as Croix-Luizet. All you have to do then is follow the tramlines as far as the station. You turn right, and take the second street on the left in the Boulevard des Belges. The Rue Massena runs at right angles to the Rue Tronchet."

"I'll make it if I possibly can. How far is it from here?"

"Five or six miles."

"I think I can manage that," I said.

Trombert said good-bye and left me. I watched him mount his bicycle and pedal away, a tall, silhouetted figure against the afternoon sun. Once more I felt desperately lonely. I stretched out on the ground and tried to sleep; but impatience and apprehension kept me awake. Soon I got up again and began to follow the course of the Rhone upstream. I must have presented a miserable and bedraggled appearance, but I was indifferent now to my tattered clothes and bleeding feet, careless even of my utter exhaustion. I had the prospect of a refuge; perhaps in one corner of my personal hell I should find at least the semblance of Paradise.

Trombert rode home quickly in some agitation. He left his bicycle in its usual place in the yard, and went round to his shop to find his wife. She was alone.

"Are you a Frenchwoman?" he asked her abruptly.

"Have you gone mad, Jean?"

"No. I'm asking you a perfectly serious question."

She said: "I'm Swiss, didn't you know?"

"This is no laughing matter. This afternoon I went to cut grass on the banks of the Rhone, near Vaux-en-Velin. I came on a French officer in a thicket by the river. He was in the last stages of exhaustion, and asked me to help him."

"Did you give him our address?"

"Certainly I did."

"And supposing he was an impostor? You know the Germans arrested three people from round here a few days ago. Their families have heard no more of them. Two men were shot in the street outside yesterday. We're running a frightful risk—"

"What does that matter? This man escaped last night from

Montluc. He was caught again this morning, and got away a second time. He was in the most appalling state. Patrols are combing all the villages to find him."

"How is he going to get here?"

"He's going to wait till it's dark. I couldn't bring him in broad daylight."

"What's his name?"

"I didn't ask him."

"Young or old?"

"Thirty, I should think. Perhaps forty. It was hard to tell."

"Where's he to sleep?" she asked.

"On the green divan in our room. There's nowhere else."

"I'll go and make up the bed."

"We must give him something to eat, too."

"There's hardly anything in the house," his wife said. "I'll see if I can get anything from the neighbours."

"Don't do that. It'd arouse their curiosity. We'll give him what we've got for now, and see about the rest later."

It seemed as if darkness would never come. I was sitting in a spinney, waiting for the sun to set. Soon the lengthening shadows would wrap roads and hedges in comforting obscurity; but they moved at a snail's pace across the grass. Numbness was creeping through my body, and my joints cracked whenever I stirred. I chewed some leaves to ease the hunger gnawing at my stomach. Light still glowed in the sky, though the trees were turning slowly to nocturnal ghosts; watching them, I began to think once more of Montluc, and the friends I had left behind there. What would happen to them?

I was pretty certain that at least five of them, including my neighbour, Jeantet, would by now have been shot as a reprisal for my escape. The sentry on his bicycle, too, had little to hope for but a firing-squad; he would in all likelihood have been the first to die. The cells would have been stripped of all the material that had helped me to escape—blankets, bedsteads, spoons, mattresses, and the rest. The baffled rage of the Gestapo would vent itself on my whole family. If I had known all this for certain, I think remorse would have broken down my last remnants of self-possession, and the Rhone would, there and then, have put an end to my misery.

And what about Gimenez? What had he done or said?

Obsessed by this thought, I began to make my way out of the bushes, and walk towards a carefully selected landmark to the right of the village. I went slowly, stumbling in holes and tramping down the tall grass. When I reached my first landmark, I made for a group of lights in the distance. If I kept straight on I was bound to hit the road to Croix-Luizet. I knew I should have to go quickly in order to reach the Rue Massena before curfew-time.

As I went on, my footsteps grew heavier; I was past caring about the pebbles and thorns which lacerated my feet.

Soon a line of trees showed up in the darkness, and a little beyond them the arch of a bridge. I remembered we had crossed a river that morning, between the two villages—a broad river with marshy banks.

What was my best course? Should I cross by the bridge, which might be guarded, or swim for it? I estimated the reserves of strength I had left, and kept to the road. A few cyclists and pedestrians were hurrying home. At their approach I would flatten myself in the ditch by the roadside. A stream of freezing and malodorous water ran at the bottom of it.

Gradually, as I approached, the ironwork of the bridge stood out more clearly. I could hear no sound of life from it; nothing was moving. Sweat ran down my face. Keep close to the handrail, I thought, and jump over at the least hint of danger. Don't look back, keep straight on.

On this resolve I began to cross the bridge. One yard, ten, fifteen; still nothing happened. Once I was across I put on a desperate spurt and ran for nearly a hundred yards. Then I collapsed, completely out of breath, in a garden beside the road.

When I had got my breath back and listened carefully for a while, I returned to the road. From Croix-Luizet onwards I stuck to the tramlines. By now walking was sheer agony. I advanced in short bursts, setting myself a point to reach, and stopping there for a moment's rest before starting again. The bursts became steadily shorter. I gritted my teeth. Go on, I told myself, you must keep moving. One last effort.

My breath was coming faster and faster, and cold sweat drenched my body. My legs were completely numb. I had a vision of myself fainting there, beside the main road. With a last desperate effort I spurred myself on.

Before my eyes, like some mirage, danced the picture of the house for which I was bound, clean and well-kept, with a soft bed, good food ready for me, and friendly faces. On I walked, through streets now, still instinctively ready to dodge the patrols. Luckily they could not have followed me far in the blackness.

I reached the tram terminus, turned right, and found myself in the Boulevard des Belges.

Here I rested for a little, hidden behind a gateway in a dark corner of the square. A slight commotion a little further down the street on the left roused me from my torpor and drove me on.

There were two cars outside Dr. Bacharach's house, and a German sentry on guard. A light shone from the first-floor window.

Mechanically I stumbled on.

I *must* find the Rue Tronchet. Second on the left in the Boulevard des Belges. I kept on, house by house, leaning against the wall every other moment to regain my strength. I passed one cross-road, then another. A man who seemed to be waiting for someone came up and grasped me by both arms.

"Thank God," he said, "you got here."

He drew me into a narrow passage. A door opened. I was dazzled by light. I saw two women standing in front of me. My head began to spin round. They gasped, and moved quickly to hold me up.

When I came to my senses again I was in bed. I looked up at the three smiling faces bent over me. Then I examined the room, with its red curtains and polished furniture. Someone gave me a hot drink. I felt soft white sheets and clean pyjamas soothing my worn body. I shut my eyes, and saw once again those grey walls, those thick, iron bars, the wretched, unkempt shadows that were my fellow-prisoners. Quickly I blinked my eyes open again, and, very gently, began to weep.

13

A fortnight later a senior railway inspector named
Duvivier left Jean Trombert's house to return to
his duties on the Lyons-Annemasse line. He was
decked out in a gleaming black uniform with green facings, and in
possession of perfectly forged documents establishing his profession and identity. He also carried a pistol loaded with nine oiled
cartridges. The same night one Professor Albert Desre crossed the
frontier into Switzerland, despite its being heavily guarded. Two
months after this, Superintendent Denis reached Bayonne; and a
week had not passed before the Spanish police arrested a French-
Canadian captain named Peter Lecoutre, near Pampluna. It was,
finally, Lieutenant Chalancey who was, at his own request, sec-
onded to the Commando Brigade, and completed his training as a
parachutist in Algeria. This was in the spring of 1944.

I had chosen this unit because it was to be the first to make a
landing in Southern France, and I was determined to take my
revenge on the enemy for all they had done to me. My hatred and
anger had grown steadily deeper and more tenacious as the weeks
and months passed by after my escape. The only way I could re-
lieve these emotions was in a fierce, hard-fought battle, where there
would be no room for mercy.

On November 18, 1944, we were engaged in a desperate struggle

206

to liberate Belfort. The Commandos, as always the spearhead of the attack, were fighting their way through the streets of Essert, an outlying village which formed the hinges of the German defence. Shells whined overhead, and the air was heavy with cordite. Bursting grenades deafened me; bullets ricocheted off walls, and above this explosive babel rose the screams of wounded men. I was elated by this deadly atmosphere, indifferent both to fear and danger, though corpses lay in dozens about the street.

Suddenly, not three paces in front of me, a German warrant officer appeared, his hands raised above his head. He had scrambled out of a hole in the wall, coughing and choking from the effects of the heavy black smoke that billowed from the burning building.

His mouth shaped one word: *"Kamerad!"*

At last I was the captor, and a German my prisoner.

He was a short, thick-set man, splashed with mud and wearing a sodden cape. He had a square head, and wore steel-rimmed glasses. *Fränzel?*

But a moment's inspection showed that it was not Fränzel. This would have been too much to hope for. Nevertheless . . .

I leapt at him, murderous with rage, my finger closing on the trigger of my pistol.

Then, for a split second only, I saw in his face that expression of desperate agony which I had known too well. I kept him covered, but slowly lowered the muzzle of my pistol. I beckoned him out of the line of fire, behind a nearby wall.

"Kein essen?" I asked him, "nothing to eat?"

"Nein." He shook his head.

Before I sent him back to the rear, I took out two bars of chocolate I had in the pocket of my denims, and pressed them into his trembling hand.

I had, in that moment, won what was perhaps my finest victory.